SUSAN COSTNER'S
GREAT
Sandwiches

Best Wishes,
Susan Costner

Also by Susan Costner

Gifts of Food
Good Friends, Great Dinners

SUSAN COSTNER'S
GREAT
Sandwiches

Sensational Recipes from
Uptown, Down Home, and Around the World

WITH CAMILLA TURNBULL

PHOTOGRAPHS BY FAITH ECHTERMEYER

Crown Publishers, Inc., New York

**The Earl of
Sandwich**

To Bobby Fizdale and
in memory of Arthur Gold,
mentors and friends
who taught me to adore
tuna on rye

Copyright © 1990 by Susan Costner
Photographs copyright © 1990 by Faith Echtermeyer
Photograph on page 44 copyright © by William Stage
Sandwich sculpture on page ii by David Gilhooly.

Published by Crown Publishers, Inc., 201 East 50th Street,
New York, New York 10022. Member of the Crown Publishing Group.

CROWN is a trademark of Crown Publishers, Inc.

Manufactured in Japan

Design by Lauren Dong

Library of Congress Cataloging-in-Publication Data

Costner, Susan.
    [great sandwiches]
    Susan Costner's great sandwiches: sensational recipes from uptown, down
home, and around the world /by Susan Costner, with Camilla Turnbull; photographs
by Faith Echtermeyer.
        1. Sandwiches.   I. Turnbull, Camilla.   II. Title.   III. Title:
Great sandwiches.
TX818.C58   1990
641.8′4 — dc20   89-77905

ISBN 0-517-57674-0

10   9   8   7   6   5   4   3   2   1

First Edition

ACKNOWLEDGMENTS

This book owes an enormous debt to many people — both chefs and friends —
who so generously shared their favorite recipes with me and introduced me
to a whole world of sandwiches I knew nothing about: Hilary Bein, Mary
Sue Millken, Susan Feniger, Birgitte Toft, The Brown Hotel in Louisville,
Kentucky, Gordon Naccarato, Michael Roberts, Anne Rosenweig, Judie Mc-
Cormick, Jody Maroni, Judy Rogers, Alice Waters, Philippa Spickerman,
Julian Serrano, Carlo Middione, Gary Danko, Jimmy Schmidt, Robert
Kinkead, Madeleine Kamman, Joyce Goldstein, Lidia Bastianich, Mitch
Pumpian, my uncle Bill Evely, Gigi Patout, Jane Benet, Eli Zabar, Law-
rence Vito, Julie and Gary Wagner, Debbie Schneider, Devon Fredericks,
Carol Field, Jim Dodge, Karen Mitchell, Sal Petrolino, Belle and Barney
Rhodes. Special thanks to Fred Hill and Erica Marcus for keeping me on
track, and to Ellen Kirby for typing.

As always, my dear friend Camilla Turnbull provided me with endless
patience and helpfulness. Her encouragement and enthusiasm mean more
than I can say.

I don't know what I would have done without the friendship and help of
Joan Comendant, a true doer-of-all-things who assisted me from beginning
to end.

This book would never have *been* without the beautiful photographs of
Faith Echtermeyer. Her *joie de vivre* kept me going as we tested and photo-
graphed over and over again. Her caring, her sensitivity, her warmth, and
her dedication to all our work together has been so remarkable that I marvel
at my enormous good fortune to have ever found her.

And finally, to my husband, Tor. There is no way to thank him enough for
all his support. He believed in me and helped in every way and continues to
tolerate each new obsession.

CONTENTS

"Roo was silent for a little while, and then he said, 'Shall we eat our sandwiches together, Tigger?' And Tigger said, 'Yes, where are they?'"

A. A. Milne, THE HOUSE AT POOH CORNER

INTRODUCTION 1

FINGER SANDWICHES 5

NEAPOLITAN SANDWICHES *10*
BROWN BREAD AND NASTURTIUM SANDWICHES *11*
NATIVE FIGS WITH BLUE CASTELLO ON TOASTED WALNUT
   BREAD *11*
WILD MUSHROOM SANDWICHES *14*
DEEP-FRIED EGGPLANT SANDWICHES *15*
CROSTINI DI FEGATINI *17*
GRILLED EGGPLANT SANDWICHES *18*
MOZZARELLA IN CARROZZA *18*
CARLO MIDDIONE'S STEAK FINGERS *19*
GRAVLAX ON WHEAT TOAST WITH QUAIL EGG AND
   OSETRA CAVIAR *22*
TARTINE OF SMOKED SALMON AND RED PEPPER COULIS *23*

UPDATED AMERICAN CLASSICS 25

JODY MARONI'S HAUT DOG *29*
SANTA FE GRILLED CHEESE WITH CHILPOTLE CHILI PUREE
   AND AVOCADO *30*

GRILLED TUNA SANDWICH   31
THANKSGIVING ON A BUN   34
FOURTH STREET GRILL'S BLT   34
LOBSTER CLUB   35
PRESSED SANDWICH   35
THE BEST BURGER   36
CAFÉ FANNY'S EGG SALAD SANDWICH   38
JIMMY SCHMIDT'S SMOKED CHICKEN AND PEPPER
    SANDWICH   39

REGIONAL FAVORITES 41

CHESAPEAKE BAY SOFT-SHELL CRAB SANDWICH   46
SHRIMP MS. ANN POOR BOY   47
CHIPPEWA SALMON SANDWICH   48
BROWN HOTEL'S HOT BROWN   50
CONEY ISLAND RED HOTS   51
PASTRAMI REUBEN   51
LOBSTER ROLL WITH LEMON AÏOLI AND ARTICHOKES   52
OYSTER LOAF   54
MUFFULETTA   55
ED DEBEVIC'S SLOPPY JOSÉ   57
ITALIAN HERO, GRINDER, OR SUBMARINE   58
UNCLE BILL'S PORK BARBECUE SANDWICH   58

"I Make a Goooood Sandwich"

Carnegie Leo at your Service

"Food at its Best"

In his 1939 *Sandwich Manual for Professionals*, Louis P. De Gouy does a cost breakdown of some fifty sandwich favorites for interested chefs and "professionals." The peanut butter sandwich is the cheapest to produce, at 3¢ a sandwich (suggested relish: gherkins). The most expensive to turn out is the deviled Smithfield ham, at 10¢ (suggested relish: chowchow), while the most cost-effective of the top fifty is the cream cheese and jelly sandwich, with a total cost of 4¢, a selling price of 25¢, and a neat profit of 83 percent (suggested relish: sweet pickles). De Gouy glimpsed a kind of culinary El Dorado in the unparalleled convenience food, but he knew his subject: "Remember that sandwiches, which are in existence to assuage the pangs of hunger, should not be made paper-thin and completely tasteless."

INTERNATIONAL SANDWICHES 61

ASPARAGUS AND EGGS SANDWICH   66
BRAZILIAN CHURRASCO STEAK SANDWICH   67
TORTA DE PAVO   69
FALAFEL PITA SANDWICH   70
PAN BAGNAT   71
MADELEINE KAMMAN'S SANDWICH MONTAGNARD   73
TAPAWICH   73
ROAST LAMB ON GARLIC NAAN WITH EGGPLANT AND ONION
    MARMALADE   74
MONTE CRISTO   75
PYNET RODSPAETTE   78
ROASTED FILLET OF BEEF WITH HORSERADISH MAYONNAISE,
    GARLIC PUREE, AND WATERCRESS ON POPPY SEED
    ROLLS   79

UNSANDWICHES 81

ELI ZABAR'S RASPBERRY TOWER OF BAGEL   82
PEANUT BUTTER SANDWICHES   83
HILARY BEIN'S ANGEL SANDWICH   86
BLACK-EYED SUSANS   90
DEBBIE SCHNEIDER'S BREAKFAST STRATA   91
FRENCH TOAST SANDWICH   92
BRIOSCIE AL GELATO   94
SOURDOUGH BREAKFAST SANDWICH WITH PEACH PECAN
    BUTTER SAUCE   95

BREADS 97

SANDWICH OR BURGER BUNS   102
BOLILLOS   103
CITY RESTAURANT'S GARLIC NAAN   104
BANNOCK BREAD   106
BRIOCHE ARCADIA   106
CORNMEAL BREAD MODEL BAKERY   107
PANE INTEGRALE CON MIELE   108
JIMMY SCHMIDT'S JALAPEÑO CHEDDAR CHEESE BREAD   110
GARY DANKO'S WALNUT BREAD   110
HERB FOCACCIA   111

SPREADS AND SAUCES 113

Aïoli   *115*
Chilpotle Puree   *115*
Uncle Bill's Barbecue Sauce   *118*
Russian Dressing   *118*
Mayonnaise   *119*
Horseradish Mayonnaise   *122*
Salsa Mayonnaise Caffè Quadro   *122*
Rémoulade Sauce   *123*
Tahini Sauce   *125*
Baba Ghanoush   *125*
Tartar Sauce   *126*
Rómesco Sauce   *126*
Clarified Butter   *127*
Avocado-Tomato Salsa   *127*

SIDE ORDERS 129

Chili con Carne   *131*
Corn Bread Pecan Stuffing   *133*
Cranberry Sauce Robert Kinkead   *133*
Spicy New Potato Salad   *134*
Ketchup   *134*
Tangy Tarheel Coleslaw   *135*
Hush Puppies   *136*
Frijoles Refritos   *136*
Madeleine Kamman's Frites à la Parisienne   *138*
Onion Rings   *139*
Tortilla Corn Chips   *140*
Saratoga Chips   *142*
Garlic Dill Pickle   *143*
Bread and Butter Pickles   *145*

INDEX 146

"After dinner we walked through the galleria, past the other restaurants and the shops with their steel shutters down, and stopped at the little place where they sold sandwiches; ham and lettuce sandwiches and anchovy sandwiches made of very tiny brown glazed rolls and only about as long as your finger. They were to eat in the night when we were hungry."

Ernest Hemingway,
A FAREWELL TO ARMS

The Lobster Club from Arcadia in
New York City.

I NTRODUCTION

We all love them, or there is at least one of them that we never get over. Sandwiches take their place in our lives early, and we never really root them out. The literature of sandwich love is not as extensive as, say, the literature of bread or eggs or wine, but it is a passionate, heartfelt history, marked by fierce parochialism, nursery greed, and an all but palpable nostalgia. Sandwiches are as American as that other British invention, apple pie. Though named for the gambling Earl of Sandwich, who wanted a ready snack at the card tables, the hand-to-mouth comestible has reached its greatest heights here, in a country dedicated to the convenient, the handy, the informal, and the speedy. We all seem to share a native enthusiasm for the meal that wants no plate, no fork, no knife. Try asking anyone for his or her childhood or current favorite and the response you get will invariably be heated, highly personal, often rapturous. Ask a crowd and you will get impassioned arguments.

"When I was a child . . . our July 4th picnic fodder was usually either cold (and homemade) Kentucky fried chicken or else a sandwich. Indeed, the American sandwich is one of the happier results of the break with Britain."

Paul Levy, OUT *TO LUNCH*

1

"In we went [to New York's Stage Delicatessen in 1947], to be insulted by our first real New York waiter. It was heaven. Combination sandwiches were unknown in Chicago and, incredible but true, Russian dressing did not exist. A Stage Special — 65 cents then, $7.90 today — was an undesirable mélange of corned beef, tongue, Swiss cheese, coleslaw and Russian dressing on three slices of rye. What can I say? There was a time I used to dream of getting married in the Stage."

James Goldman, "Confessions of a Sandwich Lover," FOOD & WINE, *February 1985*

Neither comprehensive nor definitive, this book is simply a collection of the best sandwiches I know how to make, assembled at a time when the meal-in-the-hand is experiencing a heady revival. For years a staple of menus at coffee shops, Woolworth's back-of-the-store counters, diners, and ladies' lunches, the sandwich is now for the first time making its appearance on menus of two- to three-star restaurants at lunch and even at dinner. You may have noticed these stylish newcomers — all but unrecognizable versions of the club, the grilled cheese, the lobster roll, employing a brand-new lexicon of cross-cultural raw materials, reinvented to please an audience raised on the tempting charms of the new cuisine. I wrote this book because the sandwich — always a winning idea and one of my favorite foods — looks so irresistible all dressed up in its smart new clothes.

Today's sandwich heartily recommends itself to the demands of the times. Fit for an entire meal, it is the perfect answer to the contemporary appetite for simply prepared single-dish meals to serve to family and friends. It is ideal fare for the millions of working couples, with or without children, whose busy schedules allow few hours for lengthy food preparation. It is hailed by nutritionists as *the* well-balanced meal: light on fats, heavy on complex carbohydrates, replete with the very nutrients we normally have trouble including in our diets, such as fiber and calcium, and less fattening than a full-course lunch or dinner. It is the ally of the noncook; even someone with no cooking skills can produce a great sandwich. It is a kitchen time-saver. It satisfies real hunger at a moment in culinary history when people are hungry, having sated themselves as best they could on pretty food that wasn't enough food.

If the sandwich is timely, its appeal is also eternal. It is versatile almost beyond the meaning of the word. A sandwich can be any size — modest, as in "Oh, I think I'll just have a sandwich," or tremendous, as in "Give me the deli combo, please, on rye, and go heavy on the Russian, will you." It can be hot or cold, dipped in batter and fried, grilled, toasted in special presses, and run under a broiler. The fillings, of course, are legion. In the great on-the-go tradition of every American generation, it is blessedly portable, so that we can grab it and head for the hills. Finally, it appeals to the glutton in all of us. I once asked a friend why she thought people seemed to prefer a cookie over a slice of cake or piece of pie. She thought awhile and said: "Because with a cookie you can eat the whole thing." A sandwich is like that. It's finite. It's all yours. You get to eat the whole thing.

You will notice that some of the recipes are quite detailed and long — very long, you may think, for "just a sandwich." Although I view sandwiches and sandwich making as lighthearted subjects, I believe care must be taken to ensure a great rather than a merely good result. These are not make-do meals but surprisingly delicious ones, and a little extra effort expended in shopping for best-quality ingredients and in the correct combining of the elements will pay off handsomely. No advanced techniques are necessary, just attention to the simple things of which sandwiches are made.

Even though fashion (and fillings) may change, it's my guess that the sandwich will always be with us. Composed salads, cold pasta — these may come and go, but the meal between the slices is just too good an idea to die. I know that when I was testing recipes for this book and offering sandwiches to my husband on his lunch break from the office and again as an entrée at dinnertime, he did not seem to tire of them and appeared on each occasion noticeably cheered. In fact, more than once I had the distinct impression that there was nothing he'd rather be having.

"I am fond of haute cuisine and fonder still of peasant cooking, but down deep, where all true cravings come from, I'm a sandwich man. Pastrami, roast beef, corned beef, tongue, chopped liver, cheese, salami — taken singly or in combination, dressed with coleslaw, mustard, Russian, butter, mayonnaise or nothing — these are precious things."

James Goldman, "Confessions of a Sandwich Lover," FOOD & WINE, *February 1985*

FINGER SANDWICHES

These are the savory bitefuls of bold or subtle flavor, easily managed with one hand while the other holds a drink, glass of wine, or cup of tea. I think of sandwich hors d'oeuvres and appetizers as the ultimate beginning, awakening the senses and stimulating the palate. Tea sandwiches, less robust in character, fulfill a similar function at tea. Because no one eats a lot of any one of them at a time, I find that finger sandwiches provide the perfect proving ground for new and unexpected combinations.

A lot of people get nervous about hors d'oeuvres. If you fall into this category, remember: for drinks, cheese and crackers are fine; caviar on small rounds of toast is above reproach; and if you have a bravura basket of brightly colored crudités, no one is going to flee the room in dismay. No less a partygoer than Andy Warhol believed that the most scintillating gaggle of guests could happily survive on a diet of champagne and nuts. James Beard, who opened a catering enterprise called Hors d'Oeuvre Inc. in New York City in the 1930s, later in life turned on the entire tiny-tidbit tribe ("doots," he called them finally, with contempt).

Algernon: (picking up an empty plate in horror) "Good heavens! Lane! Why are there no cucumber sandwiches?"

Oscar Wilde,
THE IMPORTANCE OF BEING EARNEST

Opposite: A quintessential tea featuring the Neapolitan (*left*) and Brown Bread and Nasturtium (*right*) sandwiches.

5

The Bookmaker

Carlo Middione's steak fingers bear an uncanny resemblance to a curiously named sandwich that caught the eye of Escoffier. James Villas in his book *American Taste* writes: "Pseudosophisticates who enjoy sneering at the great American sandwich might do well to thumb through the pages of none other than Escoffier, the distinguished French master who didn't think much about preparing dainty tea sandwiches but was fascinated enough by something called a Bookmaker to reproduce its lengthy recipe. Essentially this is an entire loaf of bread sliced in half, buttered and filled with a thick grilled steak seasoned with horseradish and mustard, wrapped in sheets of blotting paper, and squeezed tightly in a press for ½ hour. Now that is a sandwich!"

Well, he had seen too many. On the other hand, I believe that if you have the time and inclination, there *is* something memorable about a drop-dead delicious hors d'oeuvre that is out of the ordinary and freshly conceived.

The idea of having little sandwiches as an appetizer is much older than the American cocktail party. The French have long had them in the form of tartines, oven-toasted slices of bread spread with various mixtures. In Italy these become crostini, often spread with anchovy paste or chicken livers. Today's sandwich hors d'oeuvre has undergone many permutations and can contain just about anything. If you are going all out to please a large crowd, I have no wish to keep you from such provender as almond-coated chicken wings, hot and spicy nuts, dips, hams, pâtés, turkey, and a groaning cheese board. But to supplement such a spread or to go out all by themselves, I offer here a selection of the very best of the new sandwich mouthfuls.

The dainty tea sandwich has a more retiring disposition than its relative, the cocktail or first-course finger sandwich. It is an absolutely essential part of afternoon tea, a custom quintessentially English, tradition-bound, and enjoyed now mostly as a loving exercise in nostalgia. The tea ceremony can be as simple or hearty, informal or flossy as you'd like to make it. Food served at tea should reflect the spirit of the tea ceremony itself, which is a spirit of high civilization. Sandwiches for tea must therefore be made with care. This is part of their charm. They should be savored at a tempo that is leisurely and calm. By nature they are cool, refreshing, with a refinement of flavor. Properly presented, they conjure images of a sparkling silver tea service, fine bone china, Chantilly lace, the dappled shade of a great oak thrown on an emerald lawn.

Even as Marcel Proust, remembering the indelible taste of the little scalloped madeleine cakes served at tea by his aunt, was able to reconstruct an entire social milieu, so did Oscar Wilde make much of his society's teatime favorite, the cucumber sandwich. A pale and lovely thing, to be sure. But as we prepare a plateful of these as a gesture to tradition, we really must ask: Is the tea sandwich an anachronism? Ours is a speedy age; we don't have time anymore for this kind of indulgence, but the truth is that we wish we did. So tea, the whole charming, self-protective ritual of it, is enjoying something of a revival.

Cucumber, watercress, smoked salmon, potted shrimp — these were the pillars of the tea sandwich repertoire in the glory years. Have them if you insist on a period atmosphere. I feel that new life and a greater informality can be breathed into the tea party with the inclusion of some new combinations. These new entries will surely help invigorate the mood and substance of your afternoon tea.

The fillings may be innovative, but the preparation and presentation of the finger sandwich require attention to detail and custom. I remember a small tea I gave when it appeared that Devon Fredericks and I were to go into partnership and open Loaves and Fishes in Sagaponack, Long Island. At the time I hardly knew Devon, who, fresh from a rigorous course of study at London's Cordon Bleu, was my guest of honor. Some years later, when we had been through the catering wars together, she revealed that she had had some second thoughts on that occasion when, horrified, she caught a glimpse of me preparing the tea sandwiches without spreading the butter to the edges of the bread. Nor did I seem to grasp the art of trimming the edges of the sandwiches with chopped parsley. Happily, we weathered my gaffes.

Both of Devon's observations were good ones, and there are some other tricks of the trade:

For best results, hors d'oeuvres and tea sandwiches should be

"Tea at the Ritz, arriving on blue and white china, starts with sandwiches, each crustless finger striped with one of half-a-dozen constant fillings. Down in the Ritz kitchens, it takes a sandwich chef some three hours to provide the afternoon's supply. Extra long loaves are delivered daily, sliced lengthwise in twelve giant strata. Each stratum is spread with softened butter, using a broad spatula knife. Then the fillings are added. Two long slices of brown are placed on top of two long slices of white, and so on, until six great horizontal sandwiches appear in an unbroken wall. . . . The long bread wall is then sliced at one-inch intervals to produce a multitude of neat stacks of finger sandwiches."

Helen Simpson,
THE LONDON RITZ BOOK OF AFTERNOON TEA

made as near to serving time as possible. Spreads can be made in advance, since chilling enhances their flavors.

Crust helps keep the bread fresh and should be trimmed just before serving. Trim off the crust after the filling or topping is applied. Do this neatly for a clean, crisp edge. When toast is preferred, trim the crust before toasting, and spread the toast with butter and filling the moment it is done.

Open-face sandwiches dry out more quickly than those with a second piece of bread, so you should make these last.

Hors d'oeuvres and tea sandwiches generally begin with a slice of buttered bread. The butter acts as a sealer, preventing the filling from seeping into the bread and making it soggy. Be generous with the butter, making sure it extends to the edges of the bread.

Never make a sandwich with salted butter or cold butter. The butter should always be sweet (unsalted) butter that has been softened — never melted — to room temperature.

Spreads should be creamy, not soupy, and, like the butter, should extend to the edges of the bread. Keep them well chilled before making sandwiches.

Never overwhelm an hors d'oeuvre with too many flavors; one or two main ingredients are enough. Use paper-thin slices of meat, cheese, and vegetables. The only thing worse than a soggy hors d'oeuvre is one that is so loaded with topping that it drips all over you.

Keep garnishes as simple as possible — and edible. Avoid those that wilt easily.

Slice sandwiches just before serving. Experiment with different ways of cutting the bread (see illustration, opposite).

To store sandwiches, stack them in a shallow container lined with a damp kitchen towel. Place a piece of wax paper between the layers. Cover with wax paper, then another damp towel. The sandwiches will keep for several hours.

"If I am not snobbish about foods, I am not without my aversions. I believe crusts should be neatly trimmed from the sides of the bread on sandwiches (perhaps England's greatest contribution to gastronomy)."

Craig Claiborne, THE NEW NEW YORK TIMES COOKBOOK

To trim the edges with parsley, remove the crust from all sides of the sandwich and generously butter the edges of two parallel sides. Dip the buttered edges into a small saucer of finely minced parsley and shake off any excess. Apply the parsley just before serving.

To serve, line a platter with a lace or paper doily, to absorb any juices and to make a pretty presentation. Never crowd the sandwiches or stack them on the platter.

In the recipes that follow you will see that some of the heartier finger sandwiches would overpower a tea but provide excellent ballast for a drink or two; all tea sandwiches are fine as part of a selection of hors d'oeuvres but, as a group, show a special affinity for tea. Not one of the sandwiches is difficult to make, and only a few require any real cooking (unless you are baking your own bread). What they do require is some extra shopping — but isn't shopping for the freshest and most desirable ingredients one of the great pleasures of cooking?

"Then there are bread and butter sandwiches. The bread can be white, whole wheat, rye, or any kind you like, but it must be sliced very, very thin and spread very thickly with sweet butter. The sandwiches, which should be cool, not warm and runny, can be cut into fingers, diamonds, or triangles. I like them in rather hearty fingers to pack and carry on picnics. They are superb with seafood and delicious with cold chicken, cold turkey, or any cold meat — a much happier choice than rolls."

James Beard,
BEARD ON BREAD

Six ways to cut a sandwich.

NEAPOLITAN SANDWICHES

Makes 4 tea sandwiches

Cream Cheese Filling

3 ounces cream cheese
4 tablespoons peeled, seeded, chopped, and drained cucumber
1 teaspoon finely minced scallion
Salt and pepper to taste

Egg Filling

3 hard-cooked large eggs, finely chopped
3 tablespoons Mayonnaise (page 119)
1 teaspoon dry mustard
¼ teaspoon Worcestershire sauce
Salt and pepper to taste

Unsalted butter, softened
2 slices brown bread, such as whole-grain or whole wheat
2 slices black bread, such as pumpernickel or dark deli rye
2 slices white bread, such as a good pain de mie
2 ounces smoked salmon, thinly sliced
1 bunch watercress, well washed, with tough stems removed (about 1 cup)

1. In a bowl, mix the cream cheese filling ingredients.
2. In another bowl, mix the egg filling ingredients.
3. Butter 1 slice of brown bread and 1 slice of black bread on one side only. Butter the remaining bread on both sides.
4. Place the unbuttered side of brown bread on a work surface. Spread with the cream cheese filling and then the salmon. Cover with the other slice of brown bread and press firmly. Place a slice of white bread on top, add a layer of watercress, top with the other slice of white bread, and press firmly. Finally, lay the both-sides-buttered black bread on the white bread. Cover with the egg filling and top with the remaining black bread, unbuttered side up. Cut off all the crust and wrap the sandwich tightly in plastic wrap. Weight it down and refrigerate for several hours. To serve, unwrap and slice from top to bottom into 4 finger sandwiches.

BROWN BREAD AND NASTURTIUM SANDWICHES

Makes 16 tea sandwiches

8 thinly sliced pieces of Pane Integrale con Miele (page 108), or
       any good brown or black bread
    Unsalted butter, softened
4 ounces cream cheese, whipped until light
1½ cups nasturtium flowers and leaves, well washed and dried

1. Spread the bread lightly with butter, then spread half of the slices with cream cheese. Trim the crust from the bread.
2. Layer several nasturtium flowers over the cream cheese, choosing a variety of colors and making sure that some of the petals extend over the edges of the bread. Cover with the remaining slices of bread and press down gently. Cut each sandwich into 4 triangles.

The peppery nasturtium flower is a beautiful and unexpected addition to fluffy cream cheese. Perfect for a summer tea party.

NATIVE FIGS WITH BLUE CASTELLO ON TOASTED WALNUT BREAD

Serves 6

6 slices Gary Danko's Walnut Bread (page 110)
9 ounces blue castello cheese
36 small, very ripe figs, peeled and split in half
    Walnut oil

1. With all of the ingredients at room temperature, preheat the oven to 350° F. Toast the bread in the oven for 10 minutes, or until light brown.
2. Spread with the cheese, then gently mash on the figs. Return to the oven for 3 minutes, or until the cheese melts.
3. Lightly sprinkle with walnut oil, cut into halves, and serve warm with Cabernet Sauvignon.

There are certain foods just made to go together: figs, Gorgonzola cheese, and walnuts are such a combination. But rather than place them at the end of a meal, Gary Danko, the gifted chef at the Château Souverain in California's Alexander Valley, serves these sandwiches as a savory course, paired with one of the winery's great Cabernet Sauvignons.

I love the delicacy of the smaller Japanese eggplant, but for this recipe, a large, firm "American" eggplant works best.

Japanese Deep-Fried Eggplant Sandwich

Opposite: Gary Danko's Fig Sandwich is an unusual savory course.

*"Mushroom sandwiches have
been my specialty for
years."*

Alice B. Toklas

WILD MUSHROOM SANDWICHES

Makes 8 finger sandwiches

1 cup water
1 ounce dried porcini mushrooms
2 tablespoons unsalted butter
¼ cup minced shallots (about 6 to 8 large shallots)
½ pound cultivated white mushrooms, minced
½ cup dry Madeira
½ teaspoon salt
⅛ teaspoon freshly ground black pepper
4 slices good white sandwich bread
2 slices good whole wheat bread, such as Pane Integrale
    con Miele (page 108)
¼ cup Clarified Butter (page 127)

1. Bring the water to a boil, turn off the heat, and reconstitute the
dried mushrooms in it for at least 30 minutes. Using a slotted spoon,
remove the mushrooms; reserve the liquid. Carefully rinse the mushrooms under cold water to remove all dirt; pat dry and mince. Strain
the mushroom liquid through a double layer of cheesecloth or a coffee filter.
2. In a large skillet, melt the butter. When the foam dies down, add
the shallots and sauté for 3 to 4 minutes, or until tender. Add the
porcini and white mushrooms and cook over moderate heat for 10
minutes, or until all of the liquid has evaporated. Add the Madeira,
mushroom liquid, and salt and pepper and cook until all of the liquid
has again evaporated and the mixture is quite dry. Correct the
seasoning.
3. Spread 2 slices of white bread with half of the mushroom mixture.
Lay a slice of whole wheat bread on each, and cover with the remaining mushrooms. Top with the remaining white bread and press down
firmly.
4. Wipe out the skillet, then heat the clarified butter to just below the
smoking point. Over medium-high heat, brown the sandwiches on
both sides. Turn the heat down to low and weight the sandwiches
with a heavy press, or a smaller heavy skillet, and cook for 5 to 10
minutes more, or until heated through. Cut the crust from each sandwich and cut each sandwich into 4 fingers or triangles. Serve warm
with Madeira or tea.

DEEP-FRIED EGGPLANT SANDWICHES

Makes 8 sandwiches

Peanut oil, for deep frying
1 medium eggplant (about 1 pound)
Coarse salt
1 pound shelled and deveined raw shrimp
1 large egg white
1 tablespoon cornstarch
1 teaspoon salt
½ cup finely minced scallions
½ cup finely minced water chestnuts, preferably fresh
2 teaspoons finely minced fresh ginger root
½ teaspoon sugar
1 tablespoon sesame seeds, lightly toasted

Dipping Sauce
5 tablespoons freshly squeezed lemon juice
5 tablespoons dark soy sauce
3 tablespoons rice vinegar
3 teaspoons mirin (sweet sake for cooking)
1 teaspoon tamari soy sauce
1 tablespoon loose bonito flakes (optional)

1. In a saucepan, combine the sauce ingredients in the order listed and heat until warm. Let sit for 15 minutes, then strain to remove the bonito flakes. Set aside.
2. Peel the eggplant and cut into ⅜-inch-thick slices. Lightly salt the slices, and let them drain for at least one hour in a colander under a 5-pound weight (I use a sack of flour or sugar). Pat dry. If the flesh is light in color and the seeds are small, there is no need to salt and weight the eggplant.
3. Place the shrimp in the bowl of a food processor fitted with the metal blade and puree to a paste. Add the egg white, the cornstarch dissolved in a teaspoon of water, and the salt. Blend thoroughly. Turn out into a small mixing bowl and add the scallions, water chestnuts, ginger, and sugar. Mix thoroughly.
4. Spread a slice of eggplant with some of the shrimp mixture and place another eggplant slice on top to make a sandwich. Press down and cut into 4 triangles. Repeat until all of the slices are used.
5. Heat the oil in a deep fryer or wok until hot but not smoking. Fry the sandwiches, a few at a time, for 2 to 3 minutes, turning frequently to brown on all sides. Drain on paper towels, sprinkle with sesame seeds, and serve with the dipping sauce, warm or at room temperature.

People all over the world seem to enjoy eggplant sandwiches as an hors d'oeuvre. Two of my favorites come from Italy and Japan and they are as different as their countries of origin. The inspiration for the Japanese version comes from Shizuo Tsuji and Koichiro Hata's book *Practical Japanese Cooking.*

Crostini di Fegatini

CROSTINI DI FEGATINI

Makes 8 sandwiches

8 ⅓-inch-thick slices Tuscan-style bread
1 tablespoon olive oil
1 tablespoon unsalted butter
¼ cup finely chopped shallots
½ pound chicken livers, cleaned of fat and greenish bits
2 fresh sage leaves, bruised
¼ cup Marsala
2 teaspoons capers (preferably packed in salt)
  Coarse salt and black pepper to taste
1 to 2 tablespoons melted unsalted butter if needed
  Fresh sage leaves

1. Preheat the oven to 400° F. and toast the bread for 5 minutes, or until golden.
2. Heat the oil and butter in a sauté pan. When the foam has subsided, cook the shallots until soft but not browned. Add the livers and cook them quickly over medium-high heat for 3 to 4 minutes, or until crusty outside and pink inside; do not overcook them. Stir in the sage and Marsala and cook until the liquid is almost completely evaporated, scraping up all the bits that stick to the pan.
3. Transfer the mixture to a large, wide wooden bowl or a cutting board. Add the capers and chop the mixture very fine with a mezzaluna or chef's knife. (Do not use a food processor or blender, for the mixture would turn into paste very quickly.) Season with salt and a generous grind of pepper. Beat the mixture by hand to a spreadable consistency, moistening it with a little melted butter if necessary.
4. Spread mixture on the toast. Garnish with sage leaves and serve warm.

In the Italian menu, *crostini* means a "little crust" spread with some simple savory mixture. Almost always served as a first course to whet the appetite, these rustic canapés come in an endless variety. This one is my favorite.

"In any case, it's time to liberate crostini — and not just those with chicken livers — from automatic association with the canapé crowd. Let's see them not as the effete little tidbits that tide, time, and Miss Manners have made them, but as the hearty, substantial things they once were — an actual meal. Thick toasted crusts of bread brought hot to the table and lightly buttered or brushed with sweet-flavored olive oil, then thickly spread with a savory, coarse-textured mixture of seasoned chicken livers, all served with a simple salad of greens. Good... simple... easy to make."

John Thorne,
SIMPLE COOKING

This classic Italian hors d'oeuvre couldn't be simpler to prepare.

GRILLED EGGPLANT SANDWICHES

Makes 8 round sandwiches or 16 halves

1 small eggplant (about 1 pound), unpeeled but trimmed, cut
    into ⅓-inch-thick rounds (about 16 slices)
    Coarse salt
8 anchovy fillets
2 tablespoons capers
2 tablespoons chopped fresh parsley
1 teaspoon lemon juice
    Olive oil
8 ounces mozzarella (preferably buffalo mozzarella), well chilled
    and cut into 8 slices

1. Sprinkle the eggplant slices on both sides with a little coarse salt. Layer them in a nonaluminum colander and let drain for at least 1 hour. Remove the eggplant slices and pat dry.
2. In a food processor or blender, combine the anchovies, capers, parsley, and lemon juice and process until smooth.
3. Brush each side of the eggplant slices with a little olive oil. Grill the eggplant for 3 to 4 minutes per side, or until brown and soft.
4. Spread the anchovy mixture on half of the eggplant slices, cover with the cheese, and top with the remaining eggplant. Grill until the cheese is soft. If the sandwiches are large, cut them into halves or thirds. Serve at once.

These simple and unsophisticated fried cheese sandwiches from Naples are never made with butter but with fruity olive oil. The addition of anchovies, basil, and lemon makes them deliciously complete. Serve them as an appetizer, cut into bite-size pieces, with drinks before dinner.

MOZZARELLA IN CARROZZA

Serves 4

4 thick (½-inch) slices fresh mozzarella (preferably buffalo
    mozzarella) (about ½ pound)
8 ½-inch-thick slices sandwich bread, crusts trimmed
4 anchovy fillets, drained and cut into thin slivers (optional)
2 tablespoons minced fresh basil
    Zest of 1 lemon
1 cup milk
2 large eggs
    Pinch of salt
¼ cup all-purpose flour
    Olive oil for frying

1. Place 1 slice of mozzarella on each of 4 slices of bread, making sure that none of the cheese hangs over the edges.

2. In a food processor, mash the anchovies, basil, and lemon zest to a paste. Spread the anchovy mixture on the cheese. Top with the remaining bread.

3. In a wide bowl, beat the milk and eggs and soak each sandwich in the mixture for 2 minutes per side. Combine the flour and salt on a plate and dip each side of the sandwiches in it very lightly, for a thin coating. Shake off any excess flour.

4. Heat ¼ inch olive oil in a large skillet over medium-high heat. When the oil is hot, fry the sandwiches on both sides until golden, turning once. Drain on paper towels, cut into halves or quarters, and serve immediately.

CARLO MIDDIONE'S STEAK FINGERS

Serves 6 to 8

1 **round steak, 1 to 1½ inches thick**
    Salt and black pepper to taste
2 **tablespoons olive oil or butter**
3 **tablespoons Marsala**
3 **tablespoons brandy**
1 **loaf Tuscan-style bread (bastone: "stick"; not a baguette),**
    sliced in half lengthwise

1. Season the steak with salt and pepper. Heat the oil in a heavy frying pan until hot, add the steak, and sear the bottom. Lower the flame and cook for 4 to 5 minutes. Turn and sear the other side; cook for 3 to 4 minutes more. Remove the meat to a platter and keep warm.

2. Discard any oil in the pan. Deglaze the pan with the Marsala and brandy, then reduce slightly. Strain the juice onto both halves of the bread and place the steak on one slice. Cover with the remaining slice and press down firmly.

3. Butter one side of a large piece of parchment paper or butcher paper. Place the sandwich on the buttered side of the paper and wrap tightly. Place in a sandwich press (or make your own: place the wrapped sandwich on a baking sheet, cover it with another baking sheet, and put two bricks or two 5-pound sacks of flour on top), leave for 20 minutes. This will press the sandwich together so any juices soak into the bread. Unwrap the sandwich and cut into ½-inch finger-size slices.

One of the strangest of sandwich staples is eaten with great relish by Sicilians, who happily line up on the street to savor the popular indigenous specialty: a steamed spleen sandwich. The spleen is sliced paper-thin, like pastrami, and placed between pieces of bread that have been deep-fried in hot lard right there on the street. This information was passed along to me by Carlo Middione, a second-generation Sicilian-American, whose gracious and hospitable nature is everywhere evident in his San Francisco restaurant, Vivande, as well as in his book, *Food of Southern Italy*.

Carlo skipped the steamed spleen recipe and offered me another Sicilian treat. He believes, and I tend to agree, that American sandwiches all tend to taste alike when condiments such as ketchup, mustard, and mayonnaise are used to excess. He likes the simple flavors for this *au naturel*.

It is delicious with a glass of red claret.

Julian Serrano's Gravlax on Wheat Toast.

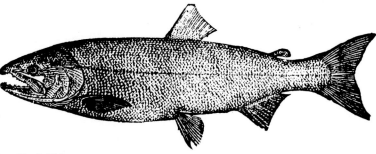

Opposite: Philippa Spickerman's Tartine of Smoked Salmon.

Julian Serrano, chef at Masa's in San Francisco, likes to call these "little starter" sandwiches. An elegant opening to a meal, they offer a combination of flavors as pleasing as their dainty appearance—all pink and yellow and pale green.

GRAVLAX ON WHEAT TOAST WITH QUAIL EGG AND OSETRA CAVIAR

Makes 16 canapés

Gravlax

- 1 1-pound salmon fillet
- 1 ounce sugar
- 1 ounce coarse salt
- 1 tablespoon cracked black pepper
- ½ bunch fresh dill
- ¼ cup brandy
- ¼ cup aquavit caraway liquor
- 2 tablespoons olive oil

Sauce

- 1 large egg
- 1 tablespoon coarse-grain mustard
- ½ cup olive oil
- 2 to 3 tablespoons gravlax marinade (see below)
- 1 tablespoon lemon juice
- ⅛ teaspoon freshly ground white pepper
- 1 tablespoon chopped fresh dill

- 4 slices wheat bread (such as Pane Integrale con Miele, page 108)
  Unsalted butter, softened
- 2 or 3 lettuce leaves (Boston or red leaf), torn into pieces
- 8 quail eggs, boiled for 3-4 minutes, rinsed, peeled, and halved
- 3 tablespoons osetra caviar
- 16 tiny dill sprigs

1. Remove the bones from the salmon but leave the skin on. Place the salmon skin side down in a long pan and cover it with the sugar, salt, pepper, dill, brandy, liquor, and oil; spread them evenly over the fish. Cover with plastic wrap and refrigerate for 3 days; turn the fish the morning of the second day. Remove the skin before slicing. Strain the marinade and reserve it for the sauce.

2. Combine the egg and mustard in the bowl of a food processor fitted with the plastic blade, or in a blender or large mixing bowl. Slowly add the oil, bit by bit, to make mayonnaise. When the sauce becomes thick, add the marinade, lemon juice, pepper, and dill. Refrigerate until ready to use.

3. Lightly toast the bread until barely golden, then lightly butter it. Using a 1-inch round cookie cutter, cut 4 rounds from each slice. Put a small piece of lettuce on each; next, a thin slice of gravlax, spread with a little sauce. Place an egg half on the sauce, then a dab of caviar on the egg. Garnish with a sprig of dill.

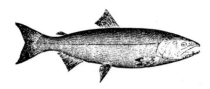

Tartine of Smoked Salmon and Red Pepper Coulis

Makes 4 sandwiches

Red Pepper Coulis *Makes 2 cups*

 5 sweet red peppers
 1 red jalapeño pepper
 1 whole garlic bulb
 1 red onion
 1 fresh rosemary or thyme sprig
 ½ cup olive oil
 3 tablespoons tomato paste
   Salt and black pepper to taste

 4 ⅓-inch-thick slices crusty Tuscan-style Italian bread, cut on the diagonal
   Olive oil
 8 ounces smoked salmon, cut on the diagonal into thin slices
   Dill sprigs

1. Preheat the oven to 400° F. Lay the peppers, garlic, onion, and rosemary in a roasting pan and pour the oil over them. Cover loosely with aluminum foil and roast in the oven for 40 minutes, or until soft.
2. Discard the rosemary. Peel, core, and seed the peppers and put them in a food processor or blender. Squeeze the soft garlic cloves out of their skins; peel the onion, and add both to the peppers, along with the tomato paste. Puree until smooth. Season with salt and pepper.
3. Brush each slice of bread with a little oil. Put the bread on a baking sheet and brown in the 400° F. oven for 4 to 5 minutes.
4. Lay the salmon on the bread. Decorate with chevrons of red pepper coulis, and garnish with dill. Cut into bite-size pieces.

When Philippa Spickerman serves these tartines at the Balboa Café in San Francisco, she lists them as an appetizer, but I could certainly enjoy them for my entire meal. The Balboa Café serves them with a crunchy salad of blanched asparagus and yellow cherry tomatoes with a balsamic vinaigrette. The colors make the plates so attractive, one scarcely has the heart to dig in.

The Egg Salad Sandwich
from Alice Waters's Café
Fanny in Berkeley.

Updated American Classics

Once upon a time, there was tuna on white. It was a good thing, a journeyman of a sandwich, hard to ruin. If you headed down to your local luncheonette, there it was on the menu, along with its sturdy brethren: peanut butter and jelly, roast beef on rye, grilled cheese and tomato, turkey club, chicken salad on white and hold the mayo, please. It was a time of supreme culinary innocence, and the tuna salad sandwich dozed on undisturbed through the decades, flanked by the obligatory pickle and sad tendril of parsley. But innocence gave way to experience, and the humble sandwich was picked up by the foodies of the eighties, who, in their frenzied search for the new, exhumed the simple fare of the home kitchen when they had sated themselves once and for all on meals of oddly shaped cold pasta and *salade composée*. Now the old specials of the lunch box and coffee shop counter are back, reinvented to suit the modern palate, the medium of expression for experimental chefs across the country. But the classics are none of them back without a difference. Each returns with a novel twist, or two or three. That traditional tuna

"When you think you have piled the buttered bread high enough, add another slice of rare beef, pastrami, roast pork, smoked salmon, turkey, salami, cheese, ham or another anchovy, sardine, prawn or egg. The only constraints you should acknowledge when stuffing the great American sandwich are those of engineering."

Paul Levy,
OUT TO LUNCH

Hold the Burger and Fries

Fast-food junkies have caught the fever. That new joint opening out there on the strip is not selling burgers or pizza. In 1988 the fastest-growing franchise in America was a newcomer called Subway Sandwiches & Salads. A shop opened every seven hours that year, according to *Venture* magazine's 1988 "Franchise 100."

PJ & B

You won't find it in *The Joy of Cooking*, and that's because it's the one single meal virtually every living breathing American knows how to make. Nor am I going to offer a recipe; I know a classic when I see one. P = peanut butter (Skippy, smooth), J = jelly (Welch's Grape), B = bread (Wonder). Do not slice on the bias, do not slice down the middle; consume whole. Plate optional.

on white reappears as grilled fresh tuna with capers and arugula on herb-flecked focaccia rubbed with olive oil and garlic. The cheeseburger reemerges with a melting Camembert center.

Well, what's better about them? you ask. The new breed is not better by virtue of excess. I'm not interested in a hot dog the length of a football field or a bedizened club sandwich top-heavy with incompatible elements. The sandwiches I've assembled are more sophisticated than that; they have made the quantum leap from brown bag to entrée. They make an excellent lunch or dinner, more vivid in flavor and more nutritious than their predecessors, and thus quite fit for company. Another thing that is better about them is the bread. Be sure to try some of the good new choices like walnut, cornmeal, and semolina. Something else that has changed: in the past, sandwiches were the cook's not-so-secret repository for food that had seen better days — in other words, leftovers. This will no longer do. Between the slices we now like to put all the bright new ingredients that are becoming part of our battery of staple foods. Just glance at the descendant of the turkey sandwich in this section. Corn bread and pecan stuffing? Mayonnaise flavored with sage? The word *leftover* would hardly spring to mind as you contemplate the attractions of this revised postholiday stand-by.

I'd like to say a word about the unvarnished originals. It is touching in a way that the old lunch counter favorites remained undiscovered so long in the American food renaissance. They were some of the last foods to fall prey to the nouvelle visionaries and, before their rediscovery, represented a bastion of conservatism and fierce consumer loyalty. Of course, the list of sandwiches varies across the country (you'll find the chili dog in one corner and the wiener with kraut in another), but regionalism plays perhaps less of a part in the standard sandwich selection than in any other section of the menu. Liverwurst, ham and cheese, fried egg sandwiches — these are indigenous everywhere, and their unprepossessing names act like charms on the digestion. These are comforting old friends, childhood companions, things we all know how to slap together from our own refrigerator flotsam. Democratic food indeed. And perhaps, when we have enjoyed sandwiches a clear cut better than these, made with more imagination and care and better raw materials, we may find that the old-timers still hang on, and the menu that featured an upgraded pesto, sun-dried tomato, and pancetta combo on semolina once again offers a BLT when the urge for the dear familiar has reasserted itself.

In the meantime, here are some glories of what must be the golden age of the great new American sandwich. If just one of them takes its place as a classic in your home, I will feel that my enthusiasm for them has been justified.

"Always it was a club sandwich, the toast brown and crisp, the turkey moist with mayonnaise, the bacon sharp and smoky. The sandwich sat in the center of the plate, each of its triangular quarters secured by a toothpick. Next to it, on a single leaf of Boston lettuce, were two small gherkins. I ate those first, getting them out of the way before starting on the milk. And then, either in solitary glory or with the kids whose families let them eat upstairs every day, I looked out over the boats rocking at their moorings and lazily worked my way through each triangle. The waiter called me 'sir,' the table cloth was white — and I was very fond of sandwiches."

Vladimir Estragon

This is Jody Maroni.

JODY MARONI'S HAUT DOG

Makes 12 to 15 sandwiches

½ cup pine nuts
¼ pound dried white kadota figs or any good large dried figs
¾ cup sweet Marsala
4 garlic cloves
½ navel orange or 2 small tangerines (optional)
1 tablespoon olive oil
2½ pounds pork butt
1 bunch cilantro, tough stems removed
¼ cup finely minced fresh parsley
1 tablespoon salt
1 tablespoon freshly ground white pepper
1 tablespoon ground coriander
½ teaspoon ground ginger
¼ pound good ham, cut into julienne (optional)
8 feet natural pork casing (found in most meat markets)
12 to 15 soft hot dog buns

1. Lightly toast the pine nuts on a baking sheet in a 350° F. oven until golden. Stem the figs and marinate them in the Marsala. Sauté the garlic in oil until crisp. Using a meat grinder with a ³⁄₁₆-inch grind plate or a food processor fitted with a steel blade, grind the pork, figs and Marsala, cilantro, garlic, orange, and parsley. Add the salt, pepper, coriander, ginger, ham, and pine nuts and mix well.
2. Prepare the casing according to package directions. Stuff the casing, making sure to remove any air pockets. Fill some, twist, fill some, and twist to form links. Refrigerate for 2 days to let the flavor develop.
3. Preheat the oven to 350° F. and bake the sausages for 15 minutes, then grill them over hot coals or in the broiler for 3 minutes per side. Serve in split and warmed buns.

Jordan Monkarsh, now known as Jody Maroni, the Sausage King of Venice, California, twisted his first sausage casing at age thirteen, in his father's butcher shop. Now he sells twenty-two fancy sausage varieties—all nitrate- and preservative-free—to Los Angeles restaurants and at his Venice stand. This is a recipe for one of his most popular, a Portuguese fig and pine nut sausage.

Classic grilled cheese with south-western fire.

SANTA FE GRILLED CHEESE WITH CHILPOTLE CHILI PUREE AND AVOCADO

Makes 2 sandwiches

2 tablespoons unsalted butter, softened
4 slices corn bread or wheat bread
4 ounces Sonoma Jack cheese
2 teaspoons Chilpotle Puree (page 115)
2 tablespoons sour cream
½ ripe avocado, thinly sliced
½ small red onion, thinly sliced
2 tablespoons cilantro leaves
   Clarified Butter (page 127)

1. Butter the bread on one side only. On the unbuttered side of 2 of the slices lay half of the cheese. Top with the puree, sour cream, avocado, onion, and cilantro. Finish with the remaining cheese and the remaining bread, buttered side up.
2. In a skillet or griddle over medium heat, grill the sandwiches in clarified butter for 8 to 10 minutes, or until golden brown on each side. Cut each sandwich in half to form 2 triangles.

GRILLED TUNA SANDWICH

Makes 4 sandwiches

12 ounces ahi tuna (3- to 4-ounce steaks) or other fresh tuna
       (see Note)
    Coarse salt
    Olive oil
2   tablespoons capers, rinsed
2   tablespoons lemon zest
2   tablespoons pitted and chopped Niçoise olives
2   tablespoons extra-virgin olive oil
    Salt and cracked black pepper to taste
4   3 x 3-inch squares Focaccia (page 111), grilled
       and split Aïoli (page 115)
    Arugula or nasturtium leaves (optional)

1. Cut the tuna into 1-inch-thick steaks, taking care to trim away the bloody, fibrous bit of meat that runs along the bone. Season the tuna with coarse salt and rub it with oil. Grill over a medium wood fire for about 1½ minutes per side, or until it is seared and cooked on the edges while remaining quite rare inside. Let cool; as it rests, it should turn to medium rare.

2. Flake the tuna gently and toss it with the capers, lemon zest, olives, extra-virgin oil, and salt and pepper. Serve at room temperature on grilled focaccia or on a chewy levain-type bread, spread generously with aïoli. Add a few leaves of peppery arugula or nasturtium, if you wish.

NOTE: Choose bright, clear, firm ahi tuna or tombo albacore. I avoid the largest fish on the market, those whose fillets or "fletches" measure 6 or more inches in breadth. Their flesh tends to be chewy and insipid compared to that of smaller fish.

The updated tuna sandwich served by Judy Rogers at San Francisco's Zuni Cafe is one of the most exciting and unusual sandwiches I've eaten. Light but intensely flavored by garlic mayonnaise, capers, and olives, it reminds me of some sublime treat one might enjoy sitting on a terrace overlooking the Mediterranean.

The Santa Fe Grilled Cheese Sandwich

*"The American sandwich —
the greatest American
sandwich, I think — is
the famous 'BLT.'...
Toasted bread, however, is
de rigueur, as are good
lettuce and mayonnaise;
and the tomatoes must be
ripe, and salted and pep-
pered. Pile the ingredients
high; a proper BLT is at
least two inches thick."*

Vladimir Estragon

Michael Roberts's Pressed Sandwich from Trumps in Los Angeles.

This is a brilliant adaptation of the classic turkey sandwich, which for many of us is the true Thanksgiving meal. Bob Kinkead, the redoubtable chef and partner of 21 Federal in Washington, D.C., and Nantucket Island, Massachusetts, has built a national reputation for his innovative ways with food. His Thanksgiving on a Bun is more than a sandwich—it is an American celebration. Plan for it while making up your Thanksgiving menu—the turkey should be roasted and the cranberry sauce, stuffing, and mayonnaise made a day ahead.

THANKSGIVING ON A BUN

Makes 1 sandwich

¼ cup **Corn Bread Pecan Stuffing** (page 133)
3 slices cob-smoked or other good bacon, diced
    Sweet Potato Fries (page 138)
2 slices sandwich bread, such as **Pane Integrale con Miele** (page 108)
    Sage Mayonnaise Robert Kinkead (page 119)
    Lettuce
3 to 4 ounces freshly roasted turkey
¼ cup **Cranberry Sauce Robert Kinkead** (page 133)

1. At sandwich time, reheat the stuffing, cook the bacon, deep fry the sweet potatoes, and grill or toast the bread.
2. Generously spread both slices of bread with mayonnaise. Place a few lettuce leaves on each. On one slice layer the stuffing, bacon, turkey, and a tablespoon of cranberry sauce. Top with the other slice of bread. Cut on the diagonal, and put the remaining cranberry sauce and the fries on the side.

A former chef at the Fourth Street Grill in Berkeley, California, Judie McCormick, created this popular and delicious version of the American classic. The bacon is cooked over an intense mesquite wood fire, but it is almost as good grilled, broiled, or fried. In the spring and summer Judie adds a chiffonade of fresh basil to the sandwich.

FOURTH STREET GRILL'S BLT

Makes 2 sandwiches

8 slices Amador County bacon or Canadian bacon, thickly sliced (see Note)
2 tablespoons homemade **Mayonnaise** (page 119)
4 slices homemade bread, toasted
2 crisp romaine lettuce leaves, washed and dried
4 slices ripe beefsteak tomatoes, or 6 slices ripe Roma tomatoes (see Note)

1. Cook the bacon lightly on each side to the desired doneness. Drain on paper towels.
2. Spread the mayonnaise on the toast. Arrange the lettuce, tomatoes, and bacon on top. Cut and serve immediately.

NOTE: Amador County bacon is available at gourmet shops.
    If tomatoes are out of season, substitute ripe avocado slices.

LOBSTER CLUB

Makes 4 sandwiches

16 slices apple-smoked bacon or any good thick-sliced bacon
12 ¼-inch-thick slices Brioche Arcadia (page 106) or egg bread
     Lemon Mayonnaise (page 119)
 2 cups crispy greens (romaine, frisée, red leaf, etc.)
 2 tomatoes, sliced
16 ounces lobster meat, sliced ½ inch thick on the bias

1. Cook the bacon until crisp; set aside and keep warm.
2. Lightly toast the brioche slices. Spread with mayonnaise. Start the layering with greens, tomato, bacon, lobster, and toast; then repeat. Cut on the diagonal and serve. Mayonnaise and tomato juice must dribble down your arms as you eat this.

The sandwich star of New York, and one that surely started the trend, is Arcadia's triple-decker lobster club, an intricate play of many luxurious textures: toasted brioche, lemon mayonnaise, very crisp bacon, vine-ripened tomatoes, and salad greens perfectly complement the meaty lobster. Chef-owner Anne Rosenzweig knows what we all really want for lunch.

PRESSED SANDWICH

Makes 1 sandwich

 3 tablespoons melted butter
 ¼ medium yellow onion, sliced
 1 8-inch length French bread (parisienne size)
 ½ chicken breast, grilled or sautéed for 3 to 4 minutes per side
     over moderate heat, then sliced
 2 ounces Brie
 2 strips thick-cut bacon, well cooked

1. In a medium frypan, combine 1 tablespoon melted butter with the onion; cook, stirring, over medium heat until the onion starts to turn pale gold. Remove from the frypan and reserve on a plate.
2. Cut out the center of the bread without cutting through the crust. Stuff the cavity with the onion, chicken, Brie, and bacon.
3. Place the frypan over low heat and add half of the remaining butter. Place the sandwich in the pan, place a second frypan on top, press down, and weight it with a brick (or something else equally heavy). Cook for 4 minutes. Remove the top frypan, add the remaining butter, and turn the sandwich over. Replace the frypan and weight, and cook for 4 minutes. Cut into 4 triangles. Accompany with straw potatoes and Dijon mustard.

Los Angeles is fast becoming known as the city of flash-in-the-pan restaurants. But L.A. is also home to Trumps on Melrose, a restaurant where for almost ten years Michael Roberts's "nouvelle down-home" culinary philosophy has endured and satisfied a sophisticated and discerning clientele. Although many items on his lunch and dinner menus reflect his avant-garde cooking style, Roberts is first and foremost a master at mixing textures and flavors. This pressed sandwich shows him at the top of his form. Layers of perfectly cooked chicken, crisp bacon, buttery sautéed onions, and creamy melted Brie make for a resounding finale to a long walk down Melrose Avenue.

The Great All-American Meal happens to be a sandwich. No, not the club, BLT, or peanut butter and jelly. The burger. A treatise could be written on its murky historical origins. One burger enthusiast, Hungarian chef Louis Szathmary, in a recent bulletin of the European quarterly of the International Wine and Food Society, concluded after thirty years of research into the European origins of the ground beef patty: "Clearly American culinary genius invented hamburger; from gastronomical, culinary and nutritional points of view, it is the most characteristic of American dishes . . . . In the end, it is easier for a French chef with a knife and an open fire to create a culinary masterpiece than it is for him to produce a perfect hamburger. This is what makes the hamburger distinctively American."

Here are a few recipes for addicts of the meal-in-the-bun on the lookout for new and unfamiliar ways to sate their burger lust. This simple recipe becomes the Best Burger when you follow all the suggestions carefully. And don't mar your beauties with cottony store-bought buns!

Start with the right beef. Most chefs agree that lean ground meat does not make a good burger. What you want to buy is freshly ground beef with a minimum of 80 percent lean and 20 percent fat. I prefer the inexpensive ground chuck to sirloin or round. All produce an equally good burger, so why not buy the less expensive!

THE BEST BURGER

Makes 4 burgers

1½ pounds ground beef
    Salt and pepper to taste
 2 tablespoons unsalted butter
 4 Sandwich or Burger Buns (page 102)
    Toppings and condiments of your choice (see margin note for suggestions)

1. Shape the beef gently into 4 patties. For the crunchiest crust and juiciest insides, handle the meat as little as possible. Do not compact it. Season with a little salt and pepper.

2. Melt the butter in a large skillet over medium heat. When the foam dies down, add the patties and cook, turning once, for a total of 10 minutes for medium-rare.

Alternatively, heat a gas grill or build a medium-hot fire, and make sure that the cooking rack is well heated before you add the patties. Cook to the desired doneness. A burger grilled over a charcoal or gas flame always has that nice smoky flavor. Broiled burgers are also good, but do not get the delicious crusty outside of grilled or sautéed burgers.

3. Cut the buns in half horizontally and warm in a low oven or lightly grill over low flames. Insert the hamburgers and serve with whatever you like.

"You can find your way across this country using burger joints the way a navigator uses stars.... We have munched Bridge Burgers in the shadow of the Brooklyn Bridge and Cable Burgers hard by the Golden Gate, Dixie Burgers in the sunny South and Yankee Doodle Burgers in the North.... We had a Capitol Burger — guess where. And so help us, in the inner courtyard of the Pentagon, a Penta Burger...."

Charles Kuralt

It's toppings that take the burger to new heights. Some of us like them with ketchup or mustard, but most of us suffer from the Madonna Syndrome: we like to dress them up with lots of stuff. Here are a few newfangled ways to go.

Of course, there is lettuce, but what about wilted spinach or Swiss chard, arugula, or radicchio? Tomatoes are a favorite, but how about ratatouille, grilled onions, peppers, or eggplant?

Or try sliced red onion, guacamole, salsa, and cilantro for some southwestern flavor. Cheeseburger fans might try some Camembert or feta. With these, a few crisp slices of bacon go nicely.

For the swells, there is caviar and sour cream, or Jeremiah Tower's famous JT burger of poached garlic and mint mayonnaise, from the Balboa Café; or, his own personal favorite, black truffles and mayonnaise.

Tapénade or olivida is a great way to add extra punch to a burger, as are nut or herb compound butters, as well as the wide range of flavored mayonnaises. In other words: anything goes.

This simple but elegant dressed-up egg salad sandwich hails from none other than Alice Waters's small, jam-packed, counter-room-only Café Fanny in Berkeley, California. Dedicated to the idea of light eating and lunch, it is a trendsetter among the new sandwich havens.

CAFÉ FANNY'S EGG SALAD SANDWICH

Makes 2 sandwiches

4　large eggs
¼　cup Mayonnaise made with champagne vinegar (page 119)
　　Salt and pepper to taste
4　slices levain or crusty country-style bread
2　sun-dried tomatoes, cut into julienne
4　salt-packed anchovies, boned and rinsed

1. Bring a quart of salted water to a boil in a medium saucepan. Add the eggs, cover, and cook over medium-high heat for 7 minutes. Drain the eggs and immerse them in cold water. Peel the cooled eggs and chop them coarsely. Combine them with the mayonnaise. Taste; add salt and pepper as needed, and perhaps more mayonnaise, depending on the desired consistency.

2. Toast the bread and, when cool, spread with the egg salad. Garnish with tomato strips and anchovies. Serve open-face, or press the sides together and cut in half.

JIMMY SCHMIDT'S SMOKED CHICKEN AND PEPPER SANDWICH

Makes 4 sandwiches

8 ¼-inch-thick slices Jimmy Schmidt's Jalapeño Cheddar
    Cheese Bread (page 110)
½ cup Mustard Mayonnaise Jimmy Schmidt (page 119)
4 thin slices raclette or Gruyère cheese
2 cups shredded smoked chicken breast
½ cup roasted, peeled, seeded, and diced red pepper
¼ cup roasted, peeled, seeded, and diced publano chili pepper
    Salt and pepper to taste
8 tablespoons (1 stick) unsalted butter, softened
    Cornichons
    Black olives
    Fire chips

1. Lay out the bread and spread with mayonnaise. Lay the cheese on 4 of the slices.
2. In a small bowl, combine the chicken and peppers, and season with salt and pepper. Cover the remaining bread with the chicken mixture. Top with the cheese-covered slices to make sandwiches.
3. Spread the top of each sandwich with butter. In a nonstick skillet over medium heat, cook each sandwich, buttered side down, and spread the top slice with butter. Cover and continue to cook for 3 minutes, or until the bottom is golden. Turn over and cook for another 3 minutes. Cut the sandwiches in half diagonally and place on a serving platter, garnished with cornichons, black olives, and fire chips (Jalapeño Potato Chips, page 142).

Jimmy Schmidt of the much-heralded Rattlesnake Club restaurants in Denver and Detroit contributed this great-tasting sandwich. It has a most interesting combination of flavors: the smoked chicken, melted cheese, and chilies are piquant and intense, and the jalapeño cheese bread ties it all together.

This sandwich feeds a family of four: the pastrami on rye from New York's Carnegie Deli.

REGIONAL FAVORITES

A man downs a hearty muffuletta sandwich in a New Orleans café while another man, in a famed New York City delicatessen, polishes off a towering hot pastrami on rye. The first man hasn't heard of the delicatessen and its fantastically proportioned fare, and the second man, who would walk from the outermost reaches of Queens for the meal he has just consumed, doesn't know a muffuletta from a hole in the ground. Of course, not every corner of the United States has its sandwich standard-bearer. I'm not aware that the Pacific Northwest or the Grain Belt or the Florida peninsula are feverishly attached to a particular local favorite. The Hawaiian Islands, once called the Sandwich Islands, unaccountably lack a dish to immortalize their former name. But, even as the nation embraces the hamburger as the Great American Sandwich (no contest; it is an institution, a way of life, and, let's face it, an outright gustatory religion), so, in some parts of the country, we carry on love affairs with a whole raft of regional kingpins.

Generally, a sandwich that is a regional favorite serves as a reliable guide to the prized edibles of that place. It says something about a region's lifestyle and traditions and features some

"If I had my life to live over, I'd live over a delicatessen."

Author unknown, in THE THIRD 637 BEST THINGS ANYBODY EVER SAID, *by* Robert Byrne

Springfield Horseshoe

Created by Steve Tomko and Joseph Schweska at the Leland Hotel in Springfield, Illinois, in 1928, this regional specialty starts with a slice of toast and can have a filling of ham, egg, hamburger, and chicken, just chicken, just ham, just egg, bacon, shrimp, or turkey and corned beef — but the sauce is the star of the show. This should be of sharp, creamy, slightly spicy cheddar cheese; a classic Welsh rabbit sauce is a good choice. When the filling has been doused with sauce, the horseshoe is topped with a second slice of toast. The name "horseshoe" was derived from the shape of the cut of ham used on the hotel's original sandwich. So far this local gem has gained no wider acceptance, but to Springfield residents it clearly ranks as that city's foremost contribution to gastronomy.

of the best that its land and waters have to offer. Think of the Chesapeake Bay soft-shell crab sandwich with its attendant paper cup of tartar sauce, enjoyed as a summer staple on Maryland, Delaware, and Virginia shores. It can be found fresh only there, because that's where the blue crabs live (and molt), and if you try it somewhere else, it won't be right. The best shrimp rolls are on the Gulf Coast, the best lobster rolls in Maine. The best tomato sandwiches in the world never make it to a restaurant. They are eaten in private, over kitchen sinks, in homes throughout New Jersey in August. So, for all these recipes, try hard in your shopping to get as close as you can to the real foods that put these sandwiches on the map in the first place. Some of my adaptations and some of the recipes from restaurants and chefs around the country allow for new components that work well within the old format (see Gigi Patout's substitution of shrimp for the more traditional oysters in her knockout version of the southern poor boy, page 47).

What are the great regional glories of the sandwich tribe? The barbecue sandwiches of the South and farther west to Texas, certainly. The hefty titans of the delicatessen trade, with sides of pickle and coleslaw. The bulging Italian-style heroes. These are the prime movers. The whole subject of barbecue (the sandwich is composed of succulent minced pork or beef dressed with a tangy sauce in a plain doughy bun) incites fierce argument; serious eaters square off over what region, what state, what city or town, or roadside joint produces the best. The heroes, always made with long Italian loaves, rely for their contents on Italian delicatessen (sliced meatballs, capocollo, prosciutto, salami, mortadella; fontina and provolone; Italian peppers and olives) and are often built to gargantuan proportions. The poor boy (or po' boy), a kind of southern-style hero employing a long French loaf, fulfills a similar catchall function. James Beard theorized that this sandwich was in all probability conceived when hungry people begged for food; it could be filled with roast beef, ham, cheeses, relishes, and sometimes fish — "as elastic in its contents as the hero is today."

The rich ethnicity of the great Jewish delicatessens in New York and Chicago makes them a supreme national treasure. These are storied places, and their towering sandwiches — the lofty salami, pastrami, corned beef, tongue, and chopped chicken liver, the peerless lox and cream cheese on a split toasted bagel — elicit from their ravenous clientele perhaps more enthusiasm than I have heard voiced for any other food, period. People are willing to go to great lengths for these outsize beauties. They are willing to drive many miles, to ride through the night. Paul Levy writes of this phenomenon in *Out to Lunch*: "In my family, ninety miles — the distance to the nearest city — was not considered excessive to drive for hot pastrami on rye." It has been said of that heart-stopping amalgam of toasted bread, corned beef, sauerkraut, and Swiss cheese, the Reuben sandwich, that it dates from an era when people ate well after the theater. The deluxe all-night New York emporium that gave its name to the Reuben is gone, but the deli mavens who still seek out the old delicatessen treasures continue at all hours of the day and night to eat very well indeed.

Certain cities are renowned for sandwiches that have little or no wider distribution. Consider the Philadelphia cheese-steak sandwich with fried onions and the Louisville Hot Brown, turkey glazed with a cheese sauce and finished off with bacon and tomatoes. A close relative of the Hot Brown is the baked Devonshire sandwich of Pittsburgh, invented at the Stratford supper club, a restaurant that had a strong English motif. It features a creamy cheddar sauce over toast with bacon and turkey. St. Louis for some reason likes a sandwich of fried calf's brains on rye with pickles and onions. Old cookbooks mention parochial offerings that, one senses, have passed out of favor in the very place they got started, overwhelmed by the brasher lures of franchise foods.

Philadelphia Cheese-steak

Together with the hoagy, this quintessential street food delicacy is Philly's great contribution to the world of sandwiches. It got its start more than fifty years ago at a sandwich stand in South Philadelphia, and today Pat's King of Steaks at Ninth and Passyunk is a leading practitioner of the cheese-steak art, reportedly sending its specialty to Frank Sinatra upon request whenever he may want it. What exactly is a cheese-steak? It is almost a thousand calories' worth of greasy, juicy sandwich composed of thinly-sliced eye round or rib eye beef, American cheese, and Italian-style bread. The beef is fried in oil, the cheese (Cheez Whiz at Pat's) is tossed on to melt when the meat is nearly done, the meat goes on the Italian bread, and the whole is topped off with fried onion slivers and a sweet or spicy sauce. Fans of the sandwich place it just under religious freedom, political independence, and culture on the list of Philadelphia's principal gifts to our society.

St. Louis Brain Drain

Would you like a brain sandwich? You are not alone if you would not. Even in St. Louis, capital of the fried-brain sandwich market, there is a dwindling number of bars and restaurants where this infamous local specialty is available. "People think brains are disgusting" is the simple explanation given by an interested *St. Louis Post-Dispatch* writer. But there *are* brain sandwich lovers. They say the fried brains are "rather like oysters or clams without the fishy odor," brown and crispy on the outside, white and tender on the inside — "the soufflé of the tavern," they rave. They like to cover them with onions and pickles and eat them on rye bread, accompanied by a stein of cold beer. Most of the brain sandwich outlets are in St. Louis's old German districts, where a thrifty, stouthearted citizenry seems to genuinely appreciate them.

Where are the Milwaukee hot chicken with Roquefort sandwich, the Los Angeles sandwich (eggs, onion, and bacon on toast), the Virginia sandwich (peanuts, ham, and cream cheese on Boston brown bread)? Gone the way of the dodo, I fear.

On the other hand, regional specials can start out locally and, by virtue of an ingenious character or sheer deliciousness, break out to a wider audience and in time gain general national acceptance. For example, the hero sandwich of the mid-Atlantic coast has now moved into both more southerly and northerly latitudes, where it is called by other names: the hoagy, the grinder, the sub. The Denver and "western" sandwiches have also escaped the confines of their place of origin and extended their range. Our population is forever uprooting and moving on, and this central fact of American life virtually ensures that your own local favorites have a shot at as yet undreamed of glory in the wider world.

My mom made this soft-shell crab sandwich.

A summer staple of tidewater Virginia and along the Chesapeake Bay waters of Maryland and Delaware. Don't overcook the crabs!

CHESAPEAKE BAY SOFT-SHELL CRAB SANDWICH

Makes 2 sandwiches

½ cup all-purpose flour
½ teaspoon salt
½ teaspoon freshly ground black pepper
4 soft-shell crabs
1 large egg, lightly beaten
½ teaspoon Tabasco sauce
1 cup cracker crumbs
  Peanut oil for deep frying
2 Sandwich or Burger Buns (page 102)
2 to 4 tablespoons Tartar Sauce (page 126)
  Lemon wedges

1. Combine the flour, salt, and pepper. Dredge the crabs well in the flour. Combine the egg and Tabasco, dip the crabs in the mixture, then roll well in cracker crumbs.

2. Heat the oil to 375° F. and cook the crabs, 2 at a time, just long enough for them to brown to a golden color. Drain on absorbent paper.

3. Warm or lightly toast the rolls and add the crabs. Top with tartar sauce and serve with lemon wedges. Accompany with shoestring potatoes or Saratoga Chips (page 142).

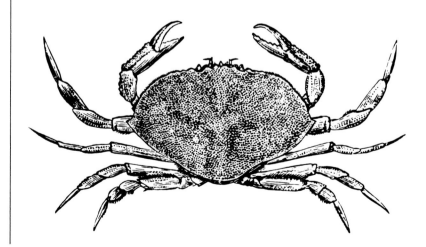

SHRIMP MS. ANN POOR BOY

Serves 6

2 pounds large shrimp, heads off
2 teaspoons salt
½ teaspoon ground red pepper
¼ teaspoon each freshly ground black and white pepper
1 cup (2 sticks) unsalted butter
¼ cup dry vermouth
½ cup lemon juice
¼ cup Worcestershire sauce
½ cup chopped scallions
½ cup chopped fresh parsley
1 loaf French bread

1. Peel and devein the shrimp. Sprinkle generously with the salt and peppers, mixing well, and arrange in a frypan or sauté pan.
2. In a saucepan, melt the butter over medium heat, add the vermouth, lemon juice, Worcestershire sauce, and scallions, and simmer over low heat for 3 minutes.
3. Pour the sauce over the shrimp and sauté them for 5 to 10 minutes, or until cooked. (This can be done in two batches; remove the cooked shrimp with a slotted spoon.)
4. Louisiana French bread has a good bit of dough, so after you cut the loaf into 6 pieces slice each piece in half, take out some of the dough. Brush on the sauce the shrimp cooked in. Heat the bread in a 350° F. oven, for 10 minutes, then fill the sandwiches with shrimp, garnish with chopped parsley, and close.

This fiery Cajun adaptation of one of the South's great traditional sandwiches was given to me by Gigi Patout of Patout's restaurant in Los Angeles. Gigi's family has cooked for generations in the storied bayou country of southern Louisiana, and her Los Angeles restaurant is the offspring of the famed Patout's of New Iberia, in the country just west of New Orleans. Gigi writes: "I like my bread heated till the crust is crispy. Lettuce and tomato may be used, but I prefer just the shrimp and bread." Co-owner André Patout adds: "The sandwich is always included in the traditional Cajun seven-course meal—one poor boy sandwich and a six-pack."

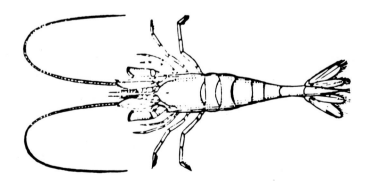

Gordon Naccarato, who features this modern version of an ancient sandwich at Gordon's, his restaurant in Aspen, Colorado, says that the fried bread originated with the Bannock Indians and was adopted by white settlers as the first campfire skillet bread of the American West. He first tasted the sandwich at the Northwest Territory food exhibit at Vancouver's Expo in 1986, then added his own touches, including the watercress mayonnaise, and has offered it regularly on his menu ever since.

Below: Gordon Naccarato's Chippewa Salmon Sandwich.

Opposite: Gigi Patout's Shrimp Ms. Ann Poor Boy.

CHIPPEWA SALMON SANDWICH

Makes 12 sandwiches, 6 servings

¼ cup extra-virgin olive oil
12 juniper berries, lightly crushed
1½ pounds fresh salmon, cut into 12 squares
1 lemon
　 Bannock Bread (page 106)
　 Watercress Mayonnaise (page 119)

1. Mix the oil and berries for a marinade. Strain half of it and reserve, and drizzle the rest over the salmon. Marinate it for 30 minutes.
2. Grill the salmon over charcoal or broil for 3 to 4 minutes per side, or until medium rare. Remove from the flame and drizzle with the strained marinade. Squeeze the lemon over the salmon. Serve on Bannock bread, cut in half horizontally and spread with mayonnaise.

The Hot Brown, the gastronomical crown jewel of Louisville, Kentucky, began as an accidental concoction in the late 1920's. A chef at the Brown Hotel piled some leftover sliced turkey breast over toast points in an ovenproof dish, covered the dish with a fluffy cheesy sauce (Mornay), and ran it under the broiler, serving the sandwich in the dish in which it was browned. Then it was garnished with two crossed strips of bacon. Later, parsley, tomato, or mushroom slivers were added as a garnish. Someone even had the ill sense to top it off with canned cling peaches. Since that time, the sandwich has metamorphosed considerably, and neo–Hot Browns have a habit of springing up all over town.

"Do not make a stingy sandwich;
Pile the cold-cuts high;
Customers should see salami;
Coming through the rye."

Alan Sherman, quoted in
OUT TO LUNCH

Brown Hotel's Hot Brown

Makes 6 sandwiches

  6 tablespoons unsalted butter
½ cup all-purpose flour
  4 cups chicken stock, heated to simmering
½ cup heavy cream
½ cup plus 2 tablespoons freshly grated Romano cheese
  2 tablespoons dry sherry
12 slices homemade white bread, crusts removed and the bread toasted and halved into triangles
1½ pounds cooked turkey breast, cut into ¼ inch slices
  3 tablespoons freshly grated Parmesan cheese
12 tomato wedges
12 strips lean bacon, cooked until crisp

1. Preheat the oven to 350° F. In a large saucepan, melt the butter over moderate heat, stir in the flour, and cook the roux over low heat for 3 minutes, stirring constantly. Remove the pan from the heat and, whisking vigorously, add the stock in a stream and bring to a boil. Stir in the cream and Romano cheese and cook over low heat, stirring, for 1 minute, or until the cheese is melted. Strain the sauce through a sieve set over a bowl and stir in the sherry.

2. Divide the toast among 6 individual gratin dishes and top with turkey slices, then the sauce.

3. Bake the dishes in the upper third of the oven for 15 minutes, or until the sauce is golden brown. Top each serving with grated Parmesan, tomato wedges, and bacon strips.

CONEY ISLAND RED HOTS

Makes 6 sandwiches

2 medium onions, finely chopped
2 tablespoons olive oil
6 hot dog buns
   Unsalted butter, softened
   Ballpark-style mustard
6 all-beef frankfurters (the best are in lamb casings), cooked
   according to package directions
   Chili con Carne (page 131), heated

1. In a frypan, sauté the onions in oil until limp.
2. Split the buns, but do not cut them all the way through. Lightly toast them. Butter them inside and spread with a little mustard. Add the frankfurters and chili. Pack some onions on top, and serve at once with cold beer.

A dog from the place where they really know how to do it. No beans in the chili, please.

"Though regarded with disdain by the chic, and horror by the alfalfa-sprout crowd, hot dogs are flat-out wonderful. And versatile. Dripping with hot onions and ball-park mustard from a Sabrett man, they taste like New York; served in little cardboard doohickeys and called frankfurters, they taste like America."

Vladimir Estragon

PASTRAMI REUBEN

Makes 1 sandwich

2 to 3 tablespoons Russian Dressing (page 118)
2 slices seeded dark rye bread
2 to 4 ounces lean pastrami, very thinly sliced
2 to 3 heaping tablespoons uncooked sauerkraut, drained
2 ounces Gruyère cheese
1 tablespoon unsalted butter

1. Spread Russian dressing on the bread. Layer the pastrami, sauerkraut, and cheese on one slice and cover with the other slice, dressing side down.
2. Melt half of the butter in a skillet and brown the sandwich until the bottom is golden. Add the remaining butter, flip the sandwich, and cook until brown and the cheese has melted. Cut in half and serve (or eat) at once, with dill pickles and coleslaw.

From the vanished Reuben's in New York City, this sandwich is more traditional when made with corned beef but oh so delicious when done with perhaps the premier deli fix, pastrami.

A hollowed-out sandwich roll has limitless possibilities. This sumptuous version is fit for a king.

LOBSTER ROLL WITH LEMON AÏOLI AND ARTICHOKES

Makes 2 sandwiches

2 Sandwich Buns (page 102), split open down the center to form a V-shaped hollow
2 tablespoons unsalted butter, softened
4 Boston lettuce leaves, washed and dried
    Lemon Aïoli (page 115)
4 to 6 ounces cooked lobster meat (from a 1- to 1½-pound lobster), coarsely chopped
¼ cup finely chopped celery
4 to 6 marinated artichoke hearts, drained and quartered
1 tablespoon coarsely chopped fresh tarragon (optional)
2 teaspoons finely chopped fresh chives

1. Spread the inside of the buns with butter. Lay 2 lettuce leaves over the butter.
2. In a small bowl, combine the aïoli, lobster, celery, artichoke hearts, and tarragon.
3. Fill the buns with the lobster mixture. Garnish with chives.

Opposite, top: The New Orleans Muffuletta

Opposite, bottom: Lobster Roll with Lemon Aïoli

Oyster loaf is a San Francisco favorite—an old, old one. This dish used to be served in restaurants all over the city but is much harder to come by now, so we who crave a good one most often make our own. The sandwich can be prepared with a standard long loaf of bread, but traditionally it is made using a round loaf. Just one of many versions, it comes from Jane Benet, food editor at the *San Francisco Chronicle*.

OYSTER LOAF

Serves 6 to 8

1 fresh round loaf sourdough French bread
½ cup (1 stick) unsalted butter
24 medium-size Pacific oysters or your favorite oysters, shucked
   Fine dry bread crumbs
   Salt and pepper to taste
   Fresh lemon juice
   Chopped fresh parsley

1. Preheat the oven to 400° F. Cut the top off the loaf of bread, about two-thirds of the way up. Scoop out the center of the loaf and of the top, leaving a 1-inch crust all around. Melt the butter and paint the inside of the loaf generously with it. Toast the loaf lightly in the oven for 5 to 10 minutes.

2. If necessary, melt more butter for the oysters. Drain the oysters, then coat them lightly with bread crumbs seasoned with salt and pepper. Fry them in butter for 4 to 5 minutes, just until they are golden and plump.

3. Layer the oysters in the loaf, sprinkling the layers lightly with lemon juice and parsley. Cover with the top of the loaf, paint the outside with butter, place on a baking sheet, and return it to the oven for 8 to 10 minutes. Serve with thin slices of dill pickle and any favorite dunking sauce for the oysters, if desired.

NOTE: To serve and eat an oyster loaf, it really is best to break it into chunks, making sure each diner gets his or her share of the plump oysters, for eating out of the hand—or use forks if you're fussy.

Muffuletta

Serves 6

1 cup pitted and chopped brine-cured green olives
1 cup pitted and chopped brine-cured black or purple olives
½ cup good olive oil
⅓ cup finely chopped fresh Italian parsley
½ cup chopped roasted peppers, peeled and seeded
2 anchovy fillets, mashed
1 teaspoon dried oregano
   Juice of ½ lemon, or to taste
   Freshly ground black pepper to taste
1 round Italian loaf, approximately 8 inches in diameter
2 cups shredded bitter greens (lettuce, arugula, or curly endive)
1½ cups chopped tomatoes (optional)
¼ pound sweet Italian salami (such as mortadella), thinly sliced
¼ pound spicy Italian hard salami (such as soppressata), thinly sliced
¼ pound provolone or Italian fontina, thinly sliced

1. In a mixing bowl, combine the olives, oil, parsley, red peppers, anchovies, oregano, lemon juice, and pepper. Cover and refrigerate overnight.

2. Cut the bread horizontally and pull out most of the soft dough in the middle. Drain the olive salad and brush both pieces of bread very generously with the marinade, using it all. Place half of the drained salad in the hollow of one piece of bread. Add layers of half of the greens tomatoes, then the sweet salami, cheese, hard salami, and remaining greens and tomatoes. Finally, heap the remaining olive salad on the other side of the loaf. Press the sides together and wrap the sandwich in plastic wrap or wax paper.

3. Put the loaf in the refrigerator, cover it with a small plate, and weight it with a 5-pound sack of flour or sugar or several pounds of unopened cans. Let it rest for at least 30 minutes, or until you are ready to serve it. Cut it into wedges.

This delicious sandwich, from down New Orleans way, is a spicy, layered combination of Italian ingredients and American *abondanza*. The olive salad's pungency is a real foil for the mild cheese and bread. You can vary the ingredients any way you choose. Only one bit of caution: don't skimp on the quality of the olives or the oil. Flavorless olives and oil will make the sandwich taste flat.

The Muffuletta

A hot and spicy hero native to New Orleans and popular throughout the state of Louisiana, traditionally it consisted of a round sesame seed loaf about 10 inches across, split in half, with various meats and cheeses, and infused with the pronounced flavors of olive salad (mostly olives, garlic, lettuce, and tomato). Filled, it should reach a height of at least 3 inches. The giant sandwich is quartered for easier handling.

Alan Skinner presents the Sloppy José at Ed Debevic's.

Ed Debevic's Short Orders Deluxe in Beverly Hills, California, is a shrine to the American sandwich. Among the offerings is one of my personal favorites: the sloppy José. Chef Mitch Pumpian serves this ground beef and Mexican spice concoction with coleslaw and a rosy-red molded gelatin salad. If this sandwich doesn't drip, it isn't authentic.

Ed debevic's sloppy josé

Makes 6 to 8 sandwiches

  ½ **cup diced onions**
  ½ **cup diced green pepper**
2½ **teaspoons minced fresh jalapeño pepper**
  1 **teaspoon minced garlic**
  2 **tablespoons olive oil or vegetable oil or butter**
  1 **pound ground prime beef (20 percent fat beef), medium grind**
  ¼ **teaspoon salt**
  ½ **teaspoon freshly ground black pepper**
  1 **teaspoon cumin**
  1 **cup ketchup**
  1 **cup diced fresh or canned tomatoes**
  6 **to 8 Sandwich or Burger Buns (page 102), lightly toasted**

1. Sauté the onions, green pepper, jalapeño pepper, and garlic in oil untill the onions are translucent. Add the beef and cook, stirring, until the meat is lightly browned. Drain off all the fat, add the salt, pepper, and cumin, and cook for 1 minute more, stirring all the time to season evenly. Add the ketchup and tomatoes and cook, uncovered, over low heat until reduced to a thick sauce.
2. Serve on toasted buns.

The gargantuan ones. In this tribe, the only unvarying component is the Italian bread. It should be 10 to 14 inches long (shaped like a submarine), split, and lightly buttered. After that, anything goes. Imitation heroes from sandwich shops are made with packaged boiled ham, shredded lettuce and, processed cheese, and they are generally pretty dreadful. Try this one instead.

ITALIAN HERO, GRINDER, OR SUBMARINE

Makes 1 large sandwich

1 tablespoon unsalted butter, softened
1 Italian sandwich loaf 10 to 14 inches long, made from hard wheat, such as Pane Integrale con Miele (page 108) or semolina
¼ cup thinly sliced mostardi frutti (mustard fruit, available in jars at Italian delicatessens)
   Small bunch arugula or radicchio
2 ounces prosciutto, thinly sliced
2 ounces cold cooked cotechino (preferably all pork), thinly sliced
2 ounces salami, thinly sliced
2 ounces provolone or Italian fontina, thinly sliced

1. Butter both halves of the loaf and spread on a layer of mostardi fruitti.
2. On the bottom half add layers of arugula, prosciutto, cotechino, salami, and provolone. Cover with the top of the loaf and press down. Cut in half or into wedges.

By birth I am half Tarheel (that is, North Carolinian), so the only meal for which I will fly clear across the country is a smoky barbecue sandwich with all the trimmings: lean, greaseless, tender, hickory-cooked pork, chopped, mixed with a little sauce, and heaped on a soft roll, served with red pepper vinegar, tangy coleslaw, and crisp hush puppies. Now there's a meal! Most of the southern states make good barbecue, but for all those really in the know, the undisputed barbecue capital of the world is North

UNCLE BILL'S PORK BARBECUE SANDWICH

Serves 6

1 5- to 6-pound picnic shoulder (shoulder of pork)
   Salt and pepper to taste

4 cups Uncle Bill's Barbecue Sauce (page 118)
1½ cups Tangy Tarheel Coleslaw (page 135)
6 Sandwich or Burger Buns, warmed (page 102)

1. Rub the meat with salt and pepper. Set aside half of the barbecue sauce for step 3. Use a large kettle-type grill with a tight-fitting lid and a mixture of hickory wood or chips and charcoal. (Bill also likes

maple wood.) Have the coals hot (about 30 to 40 minutes). When the flames have died down, add the pork, skin side up; cover with the lid and cook for 3 hours, basting several times with some of the sauce and adding more coals as needed.

2. After 3 hours, turn the pork over, cover, and cook for about 2 hours more, basting more frequently with the sauce. Make sure the fire stays hot; check the coals every hour or so. The pork is done when it easily shreds when punctured with a fork.

3. Shred 1½ pounds of the pork. Combine it with the barbecue sauce in a saucepan and heat thoroughly.

4. Spoon the meat onto one side of each split bun. Using a round scoop, mound about ¼ cup coleslaw on the meat. Top with the remaining side of the bun. Serve with more sauce on the side, crisp Hush Puppies (page 136), and a dill pickle.

"Barbecue is a touchy subject all over the country."

Calvin Trillin,
ALICE LET'S EAT

"In the early 1900s, when restaurants were gaining popularity, barbecue slowly crossed over from the church picnic and political rally to the commercial arena. Hamburger buns and sandwich bread were generally available by 1920, and within a few years there were pit barbecue stands scattered around the South dispensing prime pork sandwiches on light bread."

John Egerton, SOUTHERN FOOD

Carolina. (We're not even talking about Texas beef barbecue, a whole other incendiary subject.)

In my youth, the best places to go for good barbecue were the frequent church socials or big group affairs thrown out-of-doors by the Shriners or Masons, where they'd cook the whole pig for hours in a pit, pick it clean, mix the shredded meat with some sauce, and serve it up in a soft roll, along with a lavish spread of Brunswick stew, coleslaw, hush puppies, iced tea, and dessert. This still goes on, thank goodness. There is also a host of old commercial places in the major barbecue districts and along the back roads of the state.

Prize recipes for barbecue are jealously guarded and, once obtained, difficult to pare down for the home cook, so I am doubly proud to present you with this sandwich recipe. Believe me, it took some doing. Oddly enough, it comes not from a Tarheel but from a Virginian, my Uncle Bill, who just happens to know an awful lot about pork barbecue.

Summer visits to Uncle Bill's house in Vienna, Virginia, meant delicious barbecue. Uncle Bill would get up at the crack of dawn to fire up the coals and hickory wood on the grill. Then he'd set about making his famous sauce. No matter how hard anyone begged him for it, Bill would not give out his recipe. I tried for twenty years to pry it out of him, and it was only when I threatened to publish in this book a version by his brother Clyde that I was finally able to wrest his secret from him.

The sandwich that started
it all, roast beef on a roll.

INTERNATIONAL SANDWICHES

A sandwich by any other name tastes just as good, and sometimes better. And it does go by many other names. We would be the fools of history if we supposed that John Montagu, partaking of a snack of sliced beef between two pieces of bread in London in 1762, was the first man to eat a sandwich. His gaming-table pick-me-up gave a name to the English sandwich and introduced it to polite society, but peasants of many European countries were eating lusty meal-size sandwiches long before the word was coined. In fact, we know that loaves were baked in the Stone Age, and it is only reasonable to assume that bread wrapped around a filling antedates cutlery. Bread, either one slice or two, or a pocket or a tortilla or a bolillo, has been the sine qua non for many popular light meals for centuries throughout the world. (Well, in the Far East, you have to look rather hard. In Thailand, for instance, they simply don't eat bread. No bread, no sandwich.) The sandwich is an ancient idea and an international one. It has been with us when we needed it all along.

Historically, the international sandwich has had an air of infor-

"It has been well said that a hungry man is more interested in four sandwiches than four freedoms."

Henry Cabot Lodge, Jr.

Smörrebrod on the Fly

In Denmark, the Scandi-navian open-face sand-wich is so much a part of the fabric of everyday life that it is found in a very fresh condition in refrigerated vendomats on the streets, in railroad stations, and wherever else people are looking for something good to eat in a hurry. For a few kroner you can select from these machines a well-prepared, eye-filling crab, shrimp, anchovy and boiled egg, or liver pâté sandwich masterpiece.

mality. In most countries, custom places it in cafés or in the open air, at picnics, in the lakeside hamper, in the fields where it is pulled out for a sturdy, rustic lunch, or at the street corner, where its practical virtues as a carry-along have made it an essential prop to every mobile population.

Only recently have these convenience foods from other countries entered the hallowed realm of cuisine, and they have been taken up with a vengeance by chefs of the eighties whose clientele have survived *minceur* and are now frankly hungry enough to appreciate the sandwich for its lighthearted abundance. The chefs embrace it for its exotic allure and fresh ingredient ideas. I am delighted to include some of their stylish innovations with the international breed. In my own sandwich selection, I have chosen some plain folks and some sophisticates.

Many of our humble hero and delicatessen sandwiches are transplants from the sturdy international sandwich tradition. In her book *Everything Tastes Better Outdoors*, Claudia Roden says succinctly: "Behind the counter as part of the delicatessen trade, sandwiches . . . symbolize the Americanization of ethnic food." When we talk about international sandwiches we are talking about some great world travelers. Not surprisingly, they say a lot about the character of the people who dreamed them up and eat them all the time. Among the classics are the Mediterranean pan bagnat (or bagna or bania) and the roast beef sandwich of England. The latter started the whole modern meal-between-the-slices idea. In-fused with grainy mustard or a biting horseradish sauce, some butter, and cress, it is a sturdy staple, hard to beat. The pan bagnat, a sandwich from the south of France, has elicited praise from Arabella Boxer, Elizabeth David, and James Beard. It is, in all its many guises, a fine example of a durable sandwich that needs no improving. A baguette or pain de compagne is split open, doused with olive oil and vinegar, filled with such Niçoise bounty as anchovy fillets, capers, tomatoes, green peppers, and olives, and closed up again to marinate awhile before being eaten.

A pastoral feast or delectable beachgoing lunch, it is a supreme sampler of the best of a magical coast. The bruschetti of Italy are a close relative, rustic sandwiches of crusty, toasted, garlic-rubbed bread with extra-virgin olive oil, strewn with chopped fresh tomatoes and basil.

The flat, hollow pita of the Middle East is an obvious choice for a wide variety of street vendor specials. It is wonderful for salad-type fillings or ground beef blends—anything that might too easily escape the confines of the open-sided sandwich. In Israel, falafel-stuffed pitas are the national quick meal of choice. In Egypt, pitas are popular stuffed with chopped egg and small brown beans.

The Mexican taco and tortilla can be filled with everything form seafood to diced roast pork with chili sauce. The lesser-known torta is a true sandwich, using for bread a bobbin-shaped yeast roll called a bolillo.

Danish smörrebrod, it seems to me, are the aristocrats of the international sandwich tradition. These carefully arranged open-face delicacies have a long history behind them (originally the single slice of bread served as a plate), and it takes a serious smörrebrod maker many years to master the art of making them. There are literally hundreds of varieties, rather like a garden of innumerable but distinct brightly hued clones.

Before leaving you to the recipes, I must stress, in the manner of the real estate trade, the importance of ingredients, ingredients, ingredients. For this section I have been sparing with my suggestions for substitutions where I feel they might interfere with the integrity of the original. If you use refrigerator leftovers, if you don't take the trouble to find in your local ethnic markets (if you have them) the fresh, real, and unadulterated thing, you will have missed the point—and the surprise—of these great sandwiches from other places. If you live in a part of the country where you simply can't get most of these things, perhaps these are not the sandwiches you'd be best off trying.

The Sandwich in History

Is this how it really started? In his *Sandwich Manual for Professionals*, (1939), Louis P. De Gouy, former master chef at New York's Waldorf Astoria, theorized that the sandwich was the "invention of the great Jewish teacher, Rabbi Hillel, who lived between 70 B.C. and A.D. 70. The Jewish people during the Passover feast ritual still follow Hillel's custom of eating sandwiches made of two pieces of matzoh (unleavened bread) containing mohror (bitter herbs) and haroseth (chopped nuts and apple, to resemble the mortar of Egyptians) as a reminder of Hebrew suffering before the Deliverance from Egypt."

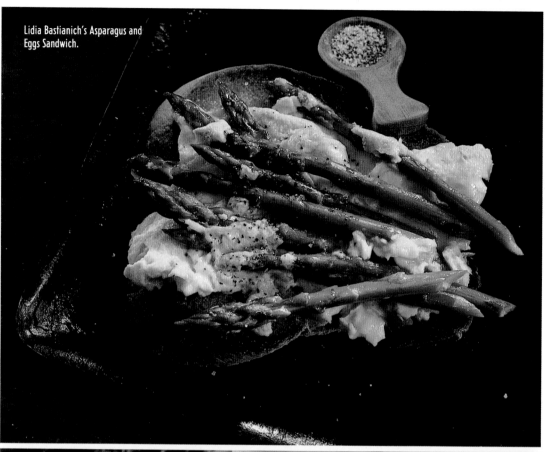

Lidia Bastianich's Asparagus and Eggs Sandwich.

The freshest ingredients make the best sandwiches.

Joyce Goldstein's Brazilian Steak
Sandwich from Caffè Quadro in
San Francisco.

Lidia Bastianich is chef and co-owner of Felidia, the esteemed Yugoslav-accented Italian restaurant on New York's Upper East Side. Her sophisticated menu and culinary style reflect the multiple influences of her native Istria, a peninsula on the Adriatic, formerly Italian, but Yugoslavian since 1946. Lidia is a woman of impressive erudition, an authority on food, anthropology, and the philosophy of taste. It is no accident that this sandwich from her childhood is strikingly simple and super-fresh.

ASPARAGUS AND EGGS SANDWICH

Makes 2 sandwiches

½ pound asparagus (preferably pencil-thin)
 4 tablespoons olive oil
    Salt and freshly ground black pepper to taste
 4 large eggs
½ loaf Italian bread

1. Wash the asparagus under cold running water. The bottom of a thick stalk is a little tough, so snap off and discard about 2 inches; you will feel the breaking point. If using the thicker asparagus, scrape the stalk to remove the tough skin, then cut the asparagus into thirds. Leave the part with the asparagus head intact; cut the other pieces, into thirds lengthwise. If the asparagus are pencil-thin, it is not necessary to scrape them, snap off the bottom, or cut lengthwise.
2. In a medium saucepan, heat the oil until just warm, not smoking. Place the asparagus in the saucepan, add ⅛ teaspoon salt, and sauté over medium heat, stirring with a long fork or just shaking the pan by the handle, for 2 minutes or so. Then cover and cook for another 2 minutes, stirring or shaking the pan occasionally.
3. Meanwhile break the eggs into a bowl and beat, adding a pinch of salt and pepper. Cut the bread in half lengthwise. Remove the soft doughy part, and toast the loaf slightly.
4. Uncover the asparagus, raise the heat slightly, and add the eggs, stirring as you would for a frittata or omelet. Cook for 1 minute, or until the eggs are set. Scoop onto the loaf and cut it in half. Enjoy with a glass of wine for a light lunch.

Brazilian churrasco steak sandwich

Serves 6

1 large yellow onion, coarsely chopped
2 large garlic cloves, coarsely chopped
½ cup lemon juice
½ teaspoon salt
½ tablespoon freshly ground black pepper
2 flank steaks, each about 1¼ pounds
Salsa Mayonnaise Caffè Quadro (page 122)
12 slices light rye bread or corn rye bread
3 avocados, thinly sliced
Romaine lettuce (optional)

1. Pulse the onion and garlic in a food processor. Add the lemon juice and pulse again. Add the salt and pepper. Pour over the steaks and marinate for an hour, turning the steaks once or twice.
2. Preheat the broiler or light a charcoal fire. Grill the steaks for a few minutes per side so that they are rare to medium-rare. Let the steaks rest a few minutes before slicing across the grain.
3. Spread mayonnaise on the bread. Put steak on half of the slices and top with avocado. Add a lettuce leaf, if you like. Top with the remaining bread. Cut the sandwich on the diagonal and serve.

Caffè Quadro, Joyce Goldstein's sleek Italian-flavored addition to her Square One restaurant in San Francisco, gave pride of place to sandwiches very early in the great sandwich revival. Her Brazilian churrasco steak sandwich is a monument to deliciousness.

José Télpin enjoys a Falafel Pita Sandwich.

TORTA DE PAVO

Makes 6 sandwiches

6   Bolillos, hard rolls, or 4-inch lengths of sourdough bread
      (page 103)
      Safflower oil or softened butter
      Chilpotle Puree (page 115)
      Frijoles Refritos, preferably made with black beans (page 136)
1½ cups shredded iceberg lettuce
12 ounces freshly roasted turkey meat, warm
      Avocado-Tomato Salsa (page 127)
6   tablespoons sour cream

1. Preheat the oven to 400° F. Cut the rolls in half horizontally and pull out some of the bread, leaving a ½-inch-thick shell. Lightly coat the inside of the rolls with a little oil or butter, and crisp them in the oven for 10 minutes.
2. For each sandwich, spread both sides of a roll with an almost translucent layer of the puree, then a layer of beans. Return the rolls to the oven for 5 minutes, or until the beans are heated through.
3. Assemble each sandwich with a little shredded lettuce, 3 ounces turkey, a heaping tablespoon of salsa, a tablespoon of sour cream, and the remaining roll half. Serve immediately, doused with more of the fiery puree.

The Mexican torta, not yet as celebrated in this country as the taco or enchilada, is an amply stuffed sandwich of central Mexico made with an elongated yeast roll. My recipe features roast turkey with frijoles refritos (black bean version) and a spirited chilpotle (smoked chili) puree on a soft, flat, oval bolillo roll. The roll can be a challenge to come by. If you can't find bolillos, substitute a length of crusty French baguette or hard rolls or sourdough bread. Diane Kennedy, who writes extensively on Mexican cooking, says of the torta: "Admittedly I am biased but this splendid, textured snack is far superior to any sandwich north of the border."

FALAFEL PITA SANDWICH

Makes 6 sandwiches

6 whole wheat or sesame seed pita breads, wrapped in foil and
    warmed in a slow oven
    Baba Ghanoush (page 125)
1½ cups shredded lettuce
2 vine-ripened tomatoes, chopped
    Tahini Sauce (page 125)

Falafel

1 cup dried chick-peas, soaked in 4 cups water overnight
½ teaspoon baking soda
1 teaspoon salt
1 large egg, lightly beaten
½ cup finely minced scallions
2 tablespoons finely minced fresh parsley
1 teaspoon ground cuminseed
1 teaspoon ground coriander
1 garlic clove, minced
1 tablespoon fresh lemon juice
    Pinch of cayenne pepper
    Freshly ground black pepper to taste
    Peanut oil for frying

1. Drain and rinse the chick-peas and pat dry. Put the chick-peas, baking soda, and salt in a food processor or blender and chop to a coarse crumb that resembles cornmeal. Do not overchop.
2. In a bowl, combine the chick-peas with the egg, scallions, parsley, cumin, coriander, garlic, lemon juice, and cayenne and black pepper. Stir to form a loose mixture. Form it into about 18 patties 2½ inches in diameter and ¾ inch thick. Do not pat down; they should be light and loose.
3. Fry the patties in batches in several inches of hot oil for 3 to 4 minutes, turning once. Remove cooked patties with a slotted spoon, drain on paper towels, and keep warm in a low oven until all are fried.
4. Warm the pitas in oven and gently split open the tops. Spread a thick layer of baba ghanoush inside. Stuff each pita with 3 falafels and some lettuce and tomato. Pour several tablespoons of tahini sauce over all, and serve at once with plenty of napkins.

Aromatic Middle Eastern falafel, a specialty welcomed in that part of the world at breakfast, lunch, or supper, is not familiar to most of us. This recipe is for a sandwich of the deep-fried spiced chick-pea patties, baba ghanoush (a rich cream of roasted eggplant), and tahini dipping sauce —a vegetarian extravaganza.

Pan bagnat

Serves 6

Dressing

¼ cup finely chopped fresh parsley
¼ cup finely chopped fresh basil
4 anchovy fillets, rinsed and patted dry
3½ tablespoons red wine vinegar
1 cup olive oil

4–6 round crusty sandwich rolls, or 1 large baguette cut into 6
pieces
1 7-ounce can oil-packed tuna, drained and flaked
1 cup peeled, seeded, and diced vine-ripe tomatoes
1 cup pitted and chopped Niçoise, Greek, or Italian olives
4 teaspoons capers, drained
1 teaspoon finely minced garlic
1 cup red and green pepper julienne
1 cup peeled, seeded, and finely chopped cucumber
1 cup minced red onion
2 large hard-cooked eggs, chopped

1. In a food processor or blender, puree the parsley, basil, anchovies, and vinegar. Add the oil in a thin stream and blend until the dressing is thick.

2. Cut the rolls in half and scoop out the insides, leaving ½-inch-thick shell.

3. Crumble the removed bread and, in a bowl, combine it with the tuna, tomatoes, olives, capers, garlic, peppers, cucumber, onion, and eggs. Bind the tuna mixture with ¼ cup of the dressing. Spread the remaining dressing generously on the rolls.

3. Heap the tuna salad on the roll bottoms. Cover with the tops and press firmly. Wrap each sandwich tightly in plastic wrap and let it rest at room temperature for at least an hour so that the bread can absorb all of the juices.

A happy marriage of all the best ingredients from the Provençal coast of the Mediterranean. This overstuffed loaf sandwich is a meal in itself. The sandwich's name is derived from the French phrase *pain baigne*, meaning "bathed bread."

Madeline Kamman's Sandwich
from the Mountains.

MADELEINE KAMMAN'S SANDWICH MONTAGNARD

Makes 2 sandwiches

 4 slices whole-grain bread
   Dijon mustard
 4 ounces prosciutto, thinly sliced
 2 ounces blue Sago or Bleu de Bresse cheese, sliced ¼-inch thick
1½ teaspoons unsalted butter
 1 ripe Bosc pear, unpeeled but cored and thinly sliced
   Salt and pepper to taste

1. Spread the bread with a thin layer of mustard, making sure that it reaches to the edges. On 2 slices of bread, arrange half of the prosciutto and the cheese. Arrange the remaining prosciutto on the remaining bread.
2. Heat the butter in a skillet and sauté the pear slices over high heat until golden. Let cool to lukewarm, season with salt and pepper, and enclose between the bread. Cut each sandwich into 2 triangles and serve.

The peppery prosciutto and creamy blue cheese give this down-home ham and cheese sandwich an uptown taste. Madeleine suggests serving this with a side order of green salad tossed with walnut oil, wine vinegar, and a few walnut halves.

TAPAWICH

Serves 4

8 large shrimp, peeled, deveined, and butterflied, tails left on
2 tablespoons Spanish olive oil
4 slices of crusty French bread, lightly toasted
  Rómesco Sauce (page 126)
  Cilantro sprigs

1. Sauté the shrimp slowly in the oil until just pink but not brown, about 5 minutes.
2. Spread about 1 tablespoon of the sauce on each slice of bread and top with 2 cooked shrimp.
3. Garnish with cilantro sprig. Serve warm.

A tapawich is a cross between a tapa—those delicious little nibbles eaten before a typical Spanish dinner—and a larger sandwich. The phrase was developed along with this dish to complement the 1989 CUNE Blanco Seco Rioja wine. Of course you may cut the sandwich in half and serve it as an appetizer.

The creative partnership of two indefatigable talents, Mary Sue Millken and Susan Feniger, gives Los Angeles some of its most imaginative food at the City Café. Their unpredictable combinations often feature Indian ingredients, as in the following recipe. Try it the next time you have leftover cooked leg of lamb. The onion marmalade and the mustard mayonnaise can be prepared a day ahead of time and refrigerated, covered, overnight; let them come to room temperature before proceeding.

ROAST LAMB ON GARLIC NAAN WITH EGGPLANT AND ONION MARMALADE

Makes 6 sandwiches

½ pound feta cheese, preferably Bulgarian (see Note)
1 cup olive oil, or as needed

Onion Marmalade

4 tablespoons unsalted butter
3 medium onions, thinly sliced
1 teaspoon salt
1 teaspoon freshly ground white pepper
⅓ cup chicken broth
1 large garlic clove, pressed

Mustard Mayonnaise

½ cup Mayonnaise (page 119)
2 tablespoons whole-grain mustard
2 tablespoons grated fresh horseradish

⅔ cup olive oil
1 medium eggplant, cut into ¼-inch-thick rounds
2 pounds cooked medium-rare leg of lamb
6 City Restaurant's Garlic Naan (page 104), pita breads, or flatbreads
2 medium tomatoes, thinly sliced

1. Place the cheese in a shallow bowl, cover with oil, cover the bowl, and refrigerate overnight.
2. Melt the butter in a large heavy skillet over medium heat. Add the onions, salt, and pepper. Cook, stirring occasionally, for 20 minutes, or until the onions are a deep golden brown. Add the broth and garlic, reduce the heat to low, and cook for 10 minutes, or until the mixture is reduced to marmalade.
3. Mix the mayonnaise, mustard, and horseradish in a small bowl.
4. Bring the cheese to room temperature. Remove it from the oil and crumble it into a small bowl.
5. Heat the ⅔ cup oil in a large heavy skillet over medium-high heat. Add the eggplant and cook in batches for 5 minutes per side, or until

softened and golden brown. Remove with a slotted spoon and drain on paper towels.

6. Preheat the oven to 350° F. Cut the lamb into thin slices. Using a serrated knife, slice the naan in half horizontally. Arrange it on a large baking sheet, cut sides up. Generously spread 6 halves with mustard mayonnaise. Cover with the eggplant and tomatoes. Spread the remaining 6 halves with onion marmalade. Top with the lamb and cheese. Cover with wet paper towels and bake for 3 minutes, or until heated through. Remove the paper towels and top each tomato-covered half with a cheese-covered half, forming sandwiches. Transfer to plates. Cut the sandwiches in half and serve immediately.

NOTE: Bulgarian feta is creamier and less salty than Greek feta. It is available at Italian, Greek, and Middle Eastern markets and some specialty food stores.

Monte cristo

Makes 6 sandwiches

  3 tablespoons Dijon mustard
  6 tablespoons crème fraîche or sour cream
 12 slices good-quality white sandwich bread with a fine crumb,
       such as homemade pain de mie or Pepperidge Farm
       sandwich bread
 12 ounces Gruyère cheese, thinly sliced
  6 ounces Black Forest ham or any good ham, thinly sliced
  4 large eggs, lightly beaten
 ½ cup (8 tablespoons) Clarified Butter (page 127)

1. Mix the mustard and crème fraîche and spread it on the bread. Cover half of the slices with layers of cheese, ham, and more cheese. Top with the remaining bread, mustard sauce side down. Press the sandwich together firmly. Trim off the crust and press down again.
2. Dip both sides of the sandwich in the eggs. In a frypan, heat the butter and cook the sandwiches for 2 to 3 minutes per side, or until the cheese is soft and the sandwich is golden brown and crusty. Cut sandwiches in half or in quarters and serve warm.

The Monte Cristo is a batter-dipped version of the deliciously crisp and crunchy croque monsieur, standard on café menus all over France. Most European countries have a variation of the classic grilled cheese sandwich. In Italy it is mozzarella en carozza, in Spain emparedados de jamon y queso. Here in America it becomes the familiar grilled cheese or untoasted ham and cheese on rye of lunch counters and diners. The Monte Cristo, a delicious blend of pressed pain de mie, best-quality ham, and Gruyère, is a particularly irresistible form of croque monsieur and leads a double life cut into small squares for hors d'oeuvres.

Mary Sue Milliken and Susan
Feniger's Roast Lamb on Garlic
Naan from their City Café in
Los Angeles.

Two smörrebrod favorites from Aquavit in New York City: Pynet Rodspaette (*top*) and the restaurant's version of steak tartare.

In Denmark they have a fascinating way with deftly composed open-face sandwiches called smörrebrod (literally, "buttered bread"), a favorite lunch or late-night-snack food. The making of these appealing specialties is considered an art form. Birgitte Toft, smörrebrod maker at New York City's two-star restaurant Aquavit, is twenty-eight years old and has been making smörrebrod for twelve years, including two years of restaurant apprenticeship in order to master all of the technique. Her pynet rodspaette ("decorated fish") sandwich with fried flounder fillet, shrimp, and caviar is a tempting example of her exacting art.

Pynet Rodspaette

Makes 4 sandwiches

All-purpose flour, seasoned with salt and pepper
4 3- to 4-ounce flounder fillets
2 large eggs, lightly beaten
   Unseasoned bread crumbs
4 tablespoons Clarified Butter (page 127)
4 slices rye-pumpernickel bread, such as Christensen or Oroweat
4 tablespoons Danish Lurpack salted butter or regular salted butter, softened
4 Boston lettuce leaves, washed and dried
16 to 24 medium shrimp, peeled, tailed, and deveined, cooked in well-salted water for 4 to 5 minutes, or just until pink
   Rémoulade Sauce (page 123)
½ lemon, cut into 4 wedges, seeds removed
3 tablespoons Danish lumpfish caviar
4 dill sprigs

1. Lightly flour the fillets. Dip them in the beaten eggs, then quickly in the bread crumbs. In a large skillet, cook the fillets (in two batches) in very hot clarified butter for 2 to 3 minutes per side. Drain on paper towels.

2. Spread the bread with butter out to the edges. Assemble each sandwich by laying a lettuce leaf over the butter, then a flounder fillet. Decorate the fish with a row of shrimp, a heaping tablespoon of rémoulade sauce, a lemon wedge, caviar, and a dill sprig. Serve on a large plate with a knife and fork.

Roasted fillet of beef with horseradish mayonnaise, garlic puree, and watercress on poppy seed rolls

Try this upscale English version of the sandwich that started it all. It's an updated combination of fillet of beef, roasted garlic puree, and piquant horseradish sauce.

Makes 6 to 8 sandwiches

1 3- to 4-pound beef fillet, trimmed
2 teaspoons Dijon mustard
  Salt and pepper to taste
5 garlic cloves, peeled
5 tablespoons unsalted butter
  Horseradish Mayonnaise (page 122)
6 to 8 poppy seed rolls
1 bunch watercress, washed, with tough stems removed

1. Preheat the oven to 500° F. Rub the outside of the fillet with mustard and lightly season with salt and pepper. Place the garlic and butter on a square of foil, season with salt and pepper, bring the edges of the foil together, and twist to seal tightly. Cook the beef and the garlic side by side in a roasting pan for 18 minutes. Turn the oven off and let the meat rest in it for 20 minutes, or until it registers 135° F. (for rare) on a meat thermometer.
2. While the meat is cooking, make the mayonnaise.
3. When the meat is done, remove it from the oven and let stand for 10 minutes. Puree the contents of the foil in a food processor or blender or by hand. Season with salt and pepper.
4. Cut the meat into paper-thin slices. Slice each roll in half horizontally and spread both halves with a thick layer of mayonnaise. Arrange several thin slices of meat on the bottom half of each roll and spoon on some garlic puree. Add several sprigs of watercress and replace the tops of the rolls. Slice the sandwiches in half with a serrated knife.

U NSANDWICHES

Not lunch box staples, not three-star dinner entrées, not picnic stalwarts or food of the trencherman — these are the unsandwiches. Sandwiches you don't think of as sandwiches. Great for breakfast, dessert, or snacks, or to suit a child's fancy. They make up a tempting subgroup, quite impossible to ignore. They've always been out there: ice-cream sandwiches and the spin-off flying saucers and Chipwiches, filled cookies such as the Oreo, split bagels with almost every luscious morning treat caught in their tight embrace. You can call them oddities, novelties, or curiosities; I like to think of them as culinary brainstorms that know no niche.

Some of the entries in this chapter may not fall within the strict definition of a sandwich — a filling with some form of bread — but they all have something of the sandwich's cheerful, obliging spirit, if not always its characteristic ease of consumption. Eli Zabar's Raspberry Tower of Bagel and cream cheese extravaganza, for instance, is a tough one to get your hands around, but lovers of the outright delicious will find a way. One of the unsandwiches is actually a casserole built on the sandwich principle: the strata

"When it comes to dessert, I'd rather have a sandwich."

Shirley Sarvis's mom, Minnie

Opposite: The Raspberry Tower of Bagel by Eli Zabar.

is layers of peasanty white bread laced with prosciutto, eggs, cheese, and pesto, baked and served as a satisfying main course for brunch or a light supper.

In the delectable arena of ice-cream-sandwich-type desserts, you cannot do better than the scrumptious amalgam from Melrose in New York of toasted angel food cake slices filled with bittersweet coffee ice cream and decorated, Jackson Pollock–style, with chocolate dribbles. Master the broscie al gelato and you're all set to make desserts your most stuffy guests will fall for.

For breakfast, my friend and former partner Devon Frederick's cream cheese and jelly French toast sandwich will melt any heart. For brunch, I love the Stanford Court's sourdough breakfast sandwich with peach pecan butter sauce.

The list can go on. As one muses on the unsandwich, one comes up with some odd things. A highly personal agenda might include the inedible human sandwich board, parading up and down wherever a man has a message; or, if you are really looking for trouble, there is always the knuckle sandwich, which needs no recipe. A lawless breed, the unsandwiches.

ELI ZABAR'S RASPBERRY TOWER OF BAGEL

Serves 2

2 freshly baked bagels, lightly toasted
4 ounces natural cream cheese, softened
¼ cup raspberry jam
   Ripe fresh raspberries

1. Using a serrated knife, cut each bagel into 4 more or less equal slices.
2. Smear cream cheese on each slice. Spread raspberry jam over the cream cheese on all but the top layer. Press some fruit into the jam, and stack the slices to form the sandwiches. Serve with good strong coffee or tea. Pass the napkins.

Eli's breakfast sandwich is a monumental tower of deliciousness. He cuts through the bagel to make 4 neat slices, then spreads each slice with natural cream cheese and his own raspberry jam. Finally, some ripe fresh berries are pressed into the jam and cheese. So simple, yet so perfect. He also makes a Tower of Bagel with cream cheese and smoked salmon.

PEANUT BUTTER SANDWICHES

Makes 1 dozen dessert sandwiches

Peanut Butter Cookies
Makes twenty-four 3-inch cookies

½ cup (1 stick) unsalted butter, softened
½ cup smooth peanut butter
½ cup granulated sugar
½ cup light brown sugar
1 large egg
½ teaspoon baking soda
2 teaspoons boiling water
1 cup all-purpose flour
½ teaspoon salt

½ cup raspberry jam, crunchy peanut butter, or 4 ounces
    semisweet chocolate melted according to directions
    (page 90)

1. Preheat the oven to 350° F. Grease 2 baking sheets.
2. In a large bowl, cream together the butter and peanut butter. Beat in the sugars, then the egg, and mix well. In a small bowl, dissolve the baking soda in the boiling water. Mix together the flour and salt. Add half of the flour to the peanut butter mixture, then the soda, then the remaining flour, combining thoroughly.
3. Drop by tablespoonfuls on the baking sheets, about 1 inch apart. Press each cookie flat with the back of a floured fork. Bake for 10 to 12 minutes, or until golden. Let cool on a wire rack.
4. To make the sandwiches, spread about 1 teaspoon of the filling of your choice on the flat side of one of the cookies. Top with a second cookie, flat side down. Repeat with the remaining cookies.

Peanut Butter Sandwich

*"Peanut butter sandwich
    made with jam
One for me and one for
    David and
A peanut butter sandwich
    made with jam
Stick, stick, stick, stick
I can think of witches good
    and bad
But the best witch that
    I have ever had
Is a peanut butter sandwich
    made with jam
Yum, yum, yum, yum."*

Raffi Singable Songs for the Very Young, produced by Raffi, © 1976 Troubadour Records, Ltd.

Hilary Bein's Angel Food Cake.

This is what you do with Hilary Bein's Angel Food Cake.

A true trompe l'oeil from creative cook Hilary Bein at Melrose Restaurant in New York City. For best results, have all ingredients on hand and measured before you begin mixing the cake.

HILARY BEIN'S ANGEL SANDWICH

Serves 8

Angel Food Cake

⁷/₈ cup large egg whites, at room temperature
¹/₈ teaspoon salt
¹/₂ teaspoon cream of tartar
⁷/₈ cup sifted sugar (sift twice)
³/₄ teaspoon vanilla extract
¹/₂ teaspoon bitter almond extract or almond extract
¹/₂ teaspoon lemon juice
³/₄ cup sifted cake flour (sift 5 times)
   Vegetable spray

Coffee Ice Cream

2 cups milk
¹/₂ cup minus 1 tablespoon sugar
¹/₂ cup finely ground coffee
6 large egg yolks
¹/₃ cup sugar
1 cup heavy cream (not ultrapasteurized), very cold

Chocolate Sauce

3 ounces fine-quality bittersweet chocolate
¹/₄ cup boiling water

1. Wash a 9×5×3-inch loaf pan and dry it thoroughly; any trace of grease will prevent the cake from rising properly. Preheat the oven to 325° F.

2. Beat the egg whites just until foamy. Add the salt and cream of tartar and continue to beat until soft peaks form. Gradually beat in the sugar, then the extracts and lemon juice. Beat until stiff peaks form.

3. Sift about one-quarter of the flour over the egg whites and fold in gently until the flour is almost incorporated. Repeat with the remaining flour, in batches. Spread the batter gently in the pan, using a rubber spatula; do not fill it to more than ¹/₂ inch from the top. Cut through the batter with a table knife several times to eliminate any air pockets. Bake the cake in the lower third of the oven for 25 to 30 minutes, or until the top is golden brown and a cake tester comes out clean. Invert the cake onto a wire rack and let cool completely.

4. To remove the cake from the pan, run a knife around the sides of the pan several times to make sure the cake is loosened. Turn the pan

upside down over a table (or cake plate) and rap it sharply several times against the table. Slowly lift the pan, shaking gently; the cake should ease out without sticking. Wrap the cake in plastic wrap until you are ready to serve. The cake keeps well and can be made up to 2 days ahead of time.

5. To make the ice cream, scald the milk and first quantity of sugar in a saucepan. Turn off the heat and stir in the coffee. Cover the pan and let steep for just 8 minutes (any longer and the flavor turns bitter); the milk should be a dark caramel color. Strain through a fine-mesh strainer, a colander lined with cheesecloth, or a coffee filter.

6. In a saucepan, whisk together the egg yolks and the ⅓ cup sugar until the yolks are pale and the sugar has dissolved. Cook over medium heat, stirring constantly with a wooden spoon, until the mixture thickens enough to coat the back of the spoon. To test, run a finger across the back of the spoon: it should leave a definite trail, without any liquid running back into the space. Immediately remove from the heat and stir in the cold cream to stop the cooking. Strain the custard through a fine-mesh strainer into a bowl. Freeze in an ice-cream maker according to the manufacturer's directions.

7. Thoroughly coat the washed and dried loaf pan with vegetable spray. Line the pan with parchment paper or wax paper. Cut a 15-inch strip of paper 1 inch wide and lay it lengthwise down the pan; it will hang over the sides. Then cut another 15-inch strip of paper 1 inch wide and lay it across the pan, overhanging the sides. The overhang will serve as handles with which to remove the ice cream from the mold. Using a large scoop, fill the pan with ice cream, straight from the freezer, and refreeze until firm. Do not let the ice cream melt before freezing or it will crystallize.

8. To remove the ice cream from the pan, run a hot knife around the sides of the pan. Dip the bottom of the pan in hot water for 30 seconds, invert the pan, and shake hard. Gently pull on the paper handles to ease out the ice cream. Wrap well in plastic wrap, then in foil, and freeze until ready to use.

9. To make the chocolate sauce, melt the chocolate in a double boiler over hot water. Pour the boiling water into a bowl and slowly pour in the chocolate, whisking constantly until smooth. If lumps form, strain the sauce. For a thinner sauce, add more water. Serve warm. If the sauce hardens during the assembly, it can be melted over hot water.

10. Using a serrated knife, cut the cake into 16 ½-inch slices. Toast the slices to a golden brown on a baking sheet under the broiler. Watch carefully.

11. To assemble, slice the ice cream into 16 1-inch-thick slices and place each between 2 cake slices to form a sandwich. Trim off any excess ice cream to make a neat edge. Place the sandwiches on dessert plates and cut each on the diagonal into 2 triangles. Drizzle with sauce and serve at once.

If you think ice cream sandwiches are limited to the raftlike soggy wafer and gummy vanilla bars in the freezer of the supermarket, you are happily mistaken. In the old days, it is true, commercial ice cream sandwiches were made with better ingredients and were pleasantly addictive (I liked the way the tips of my fingers would stick to the chocolate wafers as I went along), but the modern product is an abomination and must be forsworn. Try a homemade one instead.

Debbie Schneider's Breakfast Strata.

My Black-Eyed Susans.

How to Eat an Unsandwich

In the world of cookie sandwiches, one cookie reigns supreme: the Oreo. Nabisco, which makes it, says it's the world's most popular cookie. Invented in 1913, the Oreo is, in the words of Betty Cornfeld and Owen Edwards, authors of *Quintessence: The Quality of Having It,* "a form of personal expression. You can eat it straightforwardly as a sandwich inviolate; or you can lift the top off, eat that, then scrape the sweet white stuff off the second wafer with your front teeth, then give the bottom wafer to someone you're not that crazy about." Sounds as if they've eaten a few.

I like Oreos, but I like the cookie sandwiches given here a lot better. They share with the prototype "creme sandwich" the characteristic filled-cookie ace in the hole: they are loads of fun to eat.

BLACK-EYED SUSANS

Makes 24 cookie sandwiches

  4 ounces hazelnuts
  ¾ cup (1½ sticks) unsalted butter, chilled
  ½ teaspoon vanilla extract
  ½ cup plus 1 tablespoon sugar
    Pinch of salt
1½ cups sifted all-purpose flour
  4 ounces semisweet chocolate

1. Line 2 baking sheets with aluminum foil.

2. The nuts must be ground fine. This can be done in a food processor, a blender, or a nut grinder. If you use a processor or blender, add 1 tablespoon of sugar to keep the nuts from lumping.

3. The dough can be put together in a mixer or food processor. If using a mixer, cream the butter, then mix in the vanilla, sugar, and salt, then the flour, and finally the ground nuts, beating until mixed. If using a food processor, leave the nuts in the bowl; add the butter, cut into small pieces, and all of the other ingredients except the chocolate, and process until the dough holds together. Chill the dough for 30 minutes.

4. Preheat the oven to 350° F. Flour a pastry cloth and a rolling pin. Use only half of the dough at a time. Form it into a ball and flour it lightly. Flatten it slightly between your hands. Then roll out carefully, flouring the top, the bottom, and the rolling pin as necessary, until it is a scant ¼ inch thick.

5. You will need a round (preferably scalloped) cookie cutter that measures 1½ inches in diameter. Starting at the outside edge of the rolled-out dough, cut rounds and place them about ½ inch apart on the foil-lined sheets. Then, with a plain round cutter that measures ¾ inch in diameter, cut holes out of the middle of half of the cookies. (Save the cutout holes and the leftovers and roll them out again to make more cookies.) Bake for 10 to 12 minutes, or until the cookies are sandy-colored. Do not underbake. Transfer the cookies to racks to cool.

6. Coarsely chop the chocolate and place it in the top of a small double boiler over hot water on low heat. Cover until partly melted, then uncover and stir until completely melted. Transfer to a small shallow cup for easy handling. Or place in a microwave-safe glass measuring cup, cover, and cook at 100 percent power for 3 minutes.

7. Turn the cookies that do not have holes in them upside down. With the tip of a small spoon, place about 1 teaspoon of melted chocolate in a mound in the center of each cookie. Do not spread it out. Then place one of the cookies with a hole over the chocolate, with the undersides together. Press together lightly. The chocolate should not extend out to the edges. Repeat, sandwiching all of the cookies. Pack them in a box, with wax paper between the layers. They can be stored in a refrigerator or the freezer. If the cookies are going to stand overnight or longer, they should be wrapped airtight.

DEBBIE SCHNEIDER'S BREAKFAST STRATA

Serves 6 to 8

 1 day-old loaf peasant-style bread or French bread, cut into
       ⅓ inch-thick slices
 1 cup milk
 ½ cup mascarpone cheese
 2 ripe tomatoes, sliced
 6 ounces prosciutto, thinly sliced
 6 ounces Italian fontina cheese, thinly sliced
 ¼ cup of your favorite pesto
 4 large eggs, beaten
      Salt and pepper to taste
 1 cup heavy or whipping cream

1. One day before serving, dip the bread slices in the milk. Gently squeeze as much liquid as possible from the bread without tearing it.
2. Place half of the bread in a 12-inch-long rectangular baking dish and cover with the mascarpone, the tomatoes, prosciutto, and fontina. Drizzle sparingly with pesto. Overlap the remaining bread slices slightly. Beat the eggs with salt and pepper and pour evenly over the layers in the dish. Cover with plastic wrap and refrigerate overnight, or at least for several hours.
3. Remove the dish from the refrigerator and bring to room temperature. Preheat the oven to 350° F.
4. Drizzle the top with the cream and bake for 45 minutes to 1 hour, or until puffy and browned. Serve immediately.

A truly wonderful cook and entertainer, Debbie served this unusual dish for her son's second-birthday brunch. It would also be good for a luncheon or light supper. For best results, start this the day before you plan to have it.

Everyone loves French toast for breakfast, and most people can barely hold themselves to two pieces of it—at a minimum. So why not make a sandwich and include a layer of your favorite breakfast ingredients! The inspiration for this recipe comes from that great New York cook, Devon Fredericks.

French toast sandwich

Makes 4 sandwiches

4 large eggs
1 cup milk, half-and-half, or buttermilk
½ teaspoon ground cinnamon
   Pinch of salt
8 slices day-old sandwich bread
4 tablespoons or more cream cheese
   Filling (your choice): your favorite jam or jelly; fresh fruit, sliced and sugared to taste (strawberries, blueberries, and apricots are three favorites); a mixture of dates and chopped walnuts; or thin slices of good baked ham, such as Black Forest ham
4 tablespoons unsalted butter
   Confectioners' sugar

1. Whisk the eggs, milk, cinnamon, and salt together in a wide shallow bowl. Spread 4 slices of bread with cream cheese. Top with the filling of your choice, and cover with the remaining bread. Soak both sides of the sandwich in the egg batter for 1 to 2 minutes per side.
2. Melt 2 tablespoons butter in a heavy skillet and sauté 2 sandwiches at a time over medium heat until golden brown, turning once. Repeat with the remaining sandwiches. Cut on the diagonal and serve warm, sprinkled with confectioners' sugar.

NOTE: This is also delicious made with cinnamon raisin bread. If you use this, omit the cinnamon from the egg batter.

Opposite: Molly serves up a breakfast sandwich.

Unearthed in Palermo by my friends Gary and Julie Wagner (passionate Italophiles, inveterate world-travelers, and excellent cooks), this Sicilian ice cream sandwich is a testimonial to Italy's superior design sense.

Sicilian ice cream (gelato) is, without a doubt, some of the best in the world. And the best way to eat it is the Palermo way—on the spot in a local gelateria, where it is stuffed into a brioche-type roll called a brioscie. This slightly sweet, soft roll is deftly split three-quarters of the way through and acts as the perfect edible container, soaking up the ice cream as it slowly melts in the hot Italian sun—unlike our own model, which tends to leak its contents along the sides.

Here are two of my favorite flavors: nocciole (hazelnut) and mocha. Sicilians favor these, as well as almond and a rich dark chocolate, but you can try any one or more of your favorite flavors, homemade or parlor-made. You may never want a cone again.

BRIOSCIE AL GELATO

Makes 8 ice cream sandwiches

Gelato di Nocciole *Makes 3 cups*

> 1 **cup milk**
> 1 **cup heavy cream**
> ¼ **cup whole hazelnuts, blanched, peeled, and toasted in a**
>   **350° F. oven until golden**
> ¾ **cup sugar**
> 4 **large egg yolks**

Mocha Gelato *Makes ½ quart*

> 2 **cups milk**
> ½ **cup ground espresso**
> 4 **large egg yolks**
> ¾ **cup sugar**
> 5 **ounces semisweet baking chocolate**

> ½ **recipe Brioche Arcadia dough (page 106)**
> 1 **large egg, lightly beaten with 1 tablespoon cream or milk**

1. To make the gelato di nocciole, scald the milk and cream in a saucepan over medium heat; do not allow it to boil. In a food processor or blender, finely grind the nuts with 1 tablespoon of the sugar to prevent lumping. Steep the nuts in the milk mixture for 30 minutes—no more, or the ice cream will be bitter. (For a smooth texture, you can strain the mixture through a double layer of cheesecloth before proceeding.)

2. Beat the egg yolks with the remaining sugar until pale and thick. Drizzle in the warm milk and nut mixture, stirring all the time. Cover the bowl and refrigerate for several hours or overnight. Freeze the mixture in an ice-cream machine, following the manufacturer's directions. Remove mixture and store.

3. To make the mocha gelato, put the milk and coffee in a saucepan and bring to a boil; simmer for 5 minutes, stirring frequently. Line a strainer with several layers of cheesecloth and set it over a bowl. Pour the coffee solution into the strainer and let it drip through.

4. Beat the egg yolks and sugar in a bowl until the mixture is thick and ribbons form. Bring the coffee-flavored milk to a boil again and gradually add it to the egg mixture in a steady stream, mixing all the time.

5. Melt the chocolate in the top of a double boiler or in a microwave oven, then pour it into the milk mixture, mixing it in thoroughly with

a whisk. Let cool completely, then refrigerate until well chilled. Freeze in your ice-cream maker, following the manufacturer's directions.

6. Divide the brioche dough into 8 pieces. Shape them into 3-inch rounds and transfer to a baking sheet, spacing them about 1½ inches apart. Let rise in a draft-free place for 1 hour, or until doubled in bulk.

7. Preheat the oven to 350° F. Brush the rolls with the beaten egg and bake for 20 minutes, or until they are light and golden and one sounds hollow when tapped on the bottom. Let cool completely on a wire rack. (The brioche rolls can be prepared a day ahead, or even earlier and frozen; thaw before proceeding.)

8. To make the ice-cream sandwiches, split the rolls three-quarters of the way through and fill with a ¼-cup scoop of each gelato. Serve with the bottom half wrapped in parchment paper.

Sourdough Breakfast Sandwich with Peach Pecan Butter Sauce

Serves 2

This is the kind of breakfast that fortifies one for a big day out-of-doors—perfect in the summer, when peaches are at their best. The recipe comes from Lawrence Vito of the Stanford Court in San Francisco.

Sauce

4 ripe peaches, peeled and pitted
3 tablespoons unsalted butter
3 tablespoons brandy
2 tablespoons light brown sugar
4 tablespoons chopped toasted pecans

French Toast

4 large eggs
1 teaspoon sugar
⅓ cup milk
6 ½-inch-thick slices sourdough bread
2 tablespoons unsalted butter

1. Cut the peaches into ¼-inch-thick slices. Melt the butter in a 1-quart saucepan, add the peaches, brandy, and sugar, and cover. Stew over low heat for 5 to 10 minutes, or until the mixture is very soft. Strain through a food mill or sieve, add the pecans, and keep warm.

2. In a bowl, mix the eggs, sugar, and milk with a fork. In a shallow dish, soak the toast in the egg mixture until it is completely absorbed.

3. Melt the butter in a heavy skillet or on a griddle. Brown the bread slowly on both sides. Pour a generous amount of sauce over the French toast, and cover with more toast and sauce.

The Acme Bakery in
Berkeley, California.

B READS

"Bread," said the great *New Yorker* reporter and gourmand A. J. Liebling, "is a good medium for carrying gravy as far as the face, but it is a diluent, not an added magnificence." Much as I admire Liebling and enjoy his opinions, on this matter I could not agree with him less. Surely this serious feeder (his phrase) was not about to build a sandwich when he said it.

The first law of sandwich making reads: If you want a really good sandwich, start with good bread. This cannot be overemphasized. Your sandwich's bread is as important as the filling. By "good" bread I mean, first of all, bread that is well made — textured, flavorful, and vital with its own special character. I also mean bread that is chosen with the character of the filling in mind. It must act as a complement to what it encloses, and harmonize with the occasion as well.

I think we have gotten immeasurably wiser about bread in this country in the last fifteen years. It's a great relief that our supermarkets (once unrelieved bread wastelands, with little to offer but cottony pap on which a thin slice of ripe tomato would sink like a stone) have been improved by the inclusion of better and more diverse loaves — high-fiber whole-grain breads, glossy ba-

"I like to eat my meat in good company, Sir."

"So do I, and the best company for meat is bread. A sandwich is better company than a fool."

Unattributed, quoted in the GENTLE ART OF COOKERY, by C. F. Leyel and Olga Hartly

Etymology of a Poor Boy

No one is quite sure how this sandwich got its curious name. A jumble of clues comes down to us. One explanation goes that the legend behind the famous hero-style sandwich originated in France. The French word *pourboire* means "tip" and, expressed as a beggar's cry, was like asking for spare change for a cup of coffee. The poor boys would knock on the doors of the French convents crying, *"Pourboire."* Rather than let them go hungry, the nuns would scrape out the larder, assembling leftovers between split loaves of French bread.

gels, Syrian pitas, crusty French and Italian loaves, home-style whites, sourdoughs if one is lucky. In sophisticated urban centers the array of choices becomes mind-boggling.

Train yourself to think of the bread in a sandwich as one of its ingredients as well as its architectural base. Think of it as one of the components of a well-planned meal. It should offer flavor, texture, ballast. It should go well with what you are creating. In other words, don't always reach for the same old thing, even though that thing is delicious. Glance over the recipes in this section. Some of the breads work well with certain fillings, not so well with others. If you are doing tea, a light, close-grained pain de mie or delicate fruit bread is right; if the sandwich is the center of a picnic lunch, a leviathan French or Italian loaf with a crumb coarse enough to scrape with garlic is what you want. You don't want to put a hefty burger in a pita; pocket bread is too slight a carrier for this cargo. Pitas are better for leaky salad-type fillings that might escape out the sides of a regular two-slice sandwich. If you are having a spicy southwestern filling, a strongly flavored, gritty cornmeal bread can stand up to the fire. A Reuben sandwich is but a shadow of itself on white but springs to attention on a seeded rye. And so on. Partner your fillings with the right bread and both will take on unexpected interest and flavor.

I have written this chapter on sandwich breads because I know that, while some of you have access to a good selection of breads, many do not, and also because all of the bread recipes I have chosen to include just could not be denied—which is to say, these homemade breads are very, very good and I doubt that many purchased loaves can outdo them. Try buying a hamburger roll to equal the tasty sesame seed sandwich bun on page 102. Some of the recipes were given to me by contributing chefs, who, not surprisingly, felt that the breads played an essential part in their sandwiches' success. Use these for the sandwich for which they were intended, but try them for other fillings of your choosing, too. These recipes should give you enough ideas for wrapping up just about any filling in this book. They are varied, often worlds apart, and are meant to spur your enthusiasm for picking out what goes well with what. With apologies to Liebling, to my mind they do constitute an "added magnificence."

"If you want to make a serious sandwich, one that you can respect, start with good bread, the best you can find."

Jim Wood,
IMAGE *magazine*
(*EXAMINER,*
November 23, 1986)

The bread at Panini, a café in Berkeley.

Sandwich selection at Café Fanny in Berkeley.

Jim Dodge's sandwich buns.

Gordon Naccarato's Bannock Bread.

This recipe comes from Jim Dodge.

SANDWICH OR BURGER BUNS

Makes 12

2 packages active dry yeast
½ cup warm milk (100° F.)
½ cup warm water (100° F.)
1 tablespoon sugar
2 large eggs
2 tablespoons oil
2 cups bread flour
1 tablespoon coarse salt
  Sesame seeds

"I know some people who don't eat burgers. But I'm not sure I trust them."

Cybill Shepherd (beef ad in BON APPETIT, April 1987)

1. Sprinkle the yeast over the milk and water in the bowl of a mixer with a bread hook. Add the sugar. Let stand for ten minutes.
2. Add 1 egg and the oil and combine. Add the flour and salt. Mix at medium speed until the dough gains elasticity and cleans the side of the bowl. Leave the dough in the bowl, covered with plastic wrap, to rise in a warm place until doubled in bulk.
3. Cut the dough into 12 pieces and roll them into balls. Beat the remaining egg, brush it on the buns, sprinkle with sesame seeds, and let rise until doubled in bulk.
4. Preheat the oven to 375° F. and bake for 18 minutes, or until golden brown.

Bolillos

Makes 18

1   package (¼ ounce) active dry yeast, or ½ ounce fresh yeast
2   cups lukewarm water
1½ teaspoons salt
5   cups sifted bread flour (see Note)

1. Put the yeast in a large bowl and soften it in ¼ cup lukewarm water. When it has liquefied completely, stir in the remaining water and the salt, and stir to mix. Gradually mix in the flour to make a slightly sticky dough that comes away from the sides of the bowl. Knead the dough on a lightly floured board for 10 minutes, or until it is smooth and elastic and has lost all its stickiness. Put the dough in a buttered bowl, cover it with a clean cloth, and leave it to rise in a warm place for 2 hours, or until it has doubled in bulk. (The oven with the pilot light on is a good warm place in cold weather. This is a slow-rising dough, and it is important to allow it enough time.)
2. At the end of the rising time, punch the dough down. Cover it and let it rise for 1 hour, or until again doubled in bulk,
3. Turn the dough out onto a lightly floured board and knead it for about 5 minutes. Divide the dough in half. Roll each piece out into an oblong, about 18 x 6 inches. Roll each piece up like a jelly roll. Cut each roll into 9 slices. Pinch the ends of each slice to form a bobbin shape, and arrange on a buttered baking sheet. Cover and let the rolls rise for 1 hour, or until doubled in bulk.
4. Preheat the oven to 400°F. Brush the rolls lightly with water and bake for 30 minutes, or until golden brown.

NOTE: Bread flour has a higher percentage of hard wheat, but all-purpose flour may be substituted.

I find that bolillos, the bobbin-shaped rolls that are sold fresh twice a day in the bakeries of Mexico, are very similar to the baguettes sold in France. You can make a close approximation of the real thing with little trouble if you use a good hard-wheat flour. Bolillos are perfect for the Torta de Pavo (page 69).

This thin Indian flatbread provides a crisp counterpoint to the Roast Lamb with Eggplant and Onion Marmalade Sandwich (page 74). In fact, it is good with most savory fillings.

CITY RESTAURANT'S GARLIC NAAN

Makes 14

   1 teaspoon active dry yeast
   1 tablespoon sugar
   1 cup warm water (120° F.)
   1 cup plain yogurt
1½ teaspoons salt
      About 5 cups bread flour

   2 tablespoons olive oil
  16 garlic cloves, cut into slivers
      Additional yogurt

1. Sprinkle the yeast and sugar over warm water in the bowl of a heavy-duty mixer fitted with a dough hook; stir to dissolve. Let stand for 5 minutes, or until foamy. Mix in the yogurt and salt. Mix in enough flour, 1 cup at a time, to form a stiff dough. Knead in the mixer for 10 minutes, or until the dough is smooth and elastic. (The dough can instead be kneaded by hand.) Lightly grease a large bowl. Add the dough, turning to coat the entire surface. Cover the dough and let rise in a warm draft-free area for 1 hour, or until doubled in bulk.
2. Heat the oil in a small heavy skillet over medium heat. Add the garlic and stir for 5 minutes, or until softened.
3. Position a rack in the upper third of the oven and preheat the oven to 500° F. Place a baking tile on a large heavy baking sheet and set the sheet on the rack. Heat the tile for 30 minutes.
4. Punch down the dough. Knead it on a lightly floured surface until smooth, adding more flour to prevent sticking, if necessary. Divide the dough into 14 pieces. Shape each into a smooth ball. Flatten each ball and stretch with your fingertips into a 6-inch round.
5. Remove the baking sheet from the oven. Place 2 or 3 rounds on the hot tile, and brush lightly with yogurt. Press some of the garlic into each round. Bake for 7 minutes, or until puffed and golden brown. Repeat with the remaining rounds. Let cool completely on a wire rack.

NOTE: Naan can be baked a day in advance. Store between sheets of wax paper in an airtight container.

The tandoori oven at the City Restaurant in Los Angeles.

The traditional Indian bread for Gordon Naccarato's Chippewa Salmon Sandwich (page 48).

BANNOCK BREAD

Makes twelve 2½-inch squares

3 cups all-purpose flour
1 teaspoon salt
1 teaspoon baking powder
⅓ cup bacon drippings
1 cup minus 1 tablespoon cold water
   Vegetable oil for panfrying

1. On a pastry board, sift together the dry ingredients. Make a well in the center and add the drippings and water. Combine with a fork until moistened. Roll out the dough ¼ inch thick, and cut into 12 2½ inch squares.
2. Panfry in ¼ inch oil, turning once, until crisp. Drain on paper towels.

An essential part of the Brioscie al Gelato (page 94) as well as Arcadia's Lobster Club (page 35).

BRIOCHE ARCADIA

Makes 2 loaves

1½ cups (3 sticks) unsweetened butter, softened
¼ cup sugar
1½ teaspoons salt
4½ to 5 cups all-purpose flour
1 cup milk
2 packages (½ ounce) active dry yeast
5 large eggs

1. In a mixer with a paddle, cream together the butter, sugar, and salt. Add the flour and mix until pea-size bits form. In a saucepan, heat the milk to 90° to 100° F.; add the yeast and let proof for 5 to 10 minutes.
2. Break the eggs into a bowl and whisk lightly. Pour the eggs and milk mixture into the flour and incorporate at low speed. When everything is well mixed, gradually increase the speed and beat for 10 to 15 minutes, or until the dough wraps around the paddle and is shiny. If the dough is too sticky to handle, add a bit more flour.

3. Let the dough rise in a covered bowl for 3 hours, then punch it down. Refrigerate it, covered, overnight.

4. Divide the dough into 2 equal pieces. Shape them into loaves and place them seam side down in loaf pans. Allow to rise until doubled in volume.

5. Meanwhile, preheat the oven to 350° F. Bake the loaves for 50 minutes, or until they sound hollow when tapped. Let cool on a wire rack.

CORNMEAL BREAD MODEL BAKERY

Makes 2 loaves

2 tablespoons active dry yeast
1 cup lukewarm water
1 quart buttermilk
½ cup (8 tablespoons) melted unsalted butter
4 cups whole wheat flour
5 cups bread flour
1½ tablespoons salt
2 cups cornmeal
1 tablespoon malt or molasses
1 large egg, beaten

1. Proof the yeast in the water for 5 minutes, or until it begins to bubble. Add the buttermilk, butter, flours, cornmeal, and malt. Mix in a heavy-duty mixer with a dough hook at low speed (or mix by hand) for 5 minutes, or until smooth and elastic. Add the salt and continue mixing for 2 to 3 minutes. You may need to add more flour if the dough is too sticky to handle. Place the dough in a lightly oiled bowl, cover tightly with plastic wrap, and let rise for 1 hour, or until doubled in bulk.

2. Punch the dough down on a floured surface and knead briefly. Divide into 2 pieces; shape into loaves or ovals and let rise until doubled in bulk.

3. Preheat the oven to 375° F. Brush the bread with egg and bake for 40 to 45 minutes, or until crusty and golden. Let cool completely on a wire rack.

My small town of St. Helena, California, population 5,000, has one of the best bakeries on the West Coast. Owner Karen Mitchell keeps us all fighting the battle of the bulge.

This recipe is from Carol Field's fabulous book *The Italian Baker*. It is one of the best whole wheat breads you can make.

PANE INTEGRALE CON MIELE

Makes 1 loaf

Starter (optional)

¼ teaspoon active dry yeast
⅔ cup lukewarm water
1½ cups unbleached all-purpose flour

Dough

1¾ teaspoons active dry yeast or ⅔ small cake (⅓ ounce) fresh
   yeast
1 tablespoon plus 2 teaspoons honey
1½ cups warm water
3¾ cups whole wheat flour
1½ teaspoons salt

1. To make the starter, stir the yeast into the water in a medium mixing bowl; let stand for 10 minutes, or until creamy. Stir in the flour with 70 to 100 strokes of a wooden spoon. Let rise, covered, for 6 to 24 hours. Measure out ¼ cup for this recipe.

NOTE: The starter freezes well and needs only about three hours at room temperature until it is bubbly and active again. It also can be refrigerated for about one week.

2. To make the dough, stir the yeast and honey into ¼ cup of the water in a large mixing bowl; let stand for 10 minutes, or until foamy. Chop the starter into small pieces and add to the dissolved yeast. Pour in the remaining water and squeeze the starter between your fingers until it is in little shreds and the water is chalky. Mix the flour and salt, and stir 1 cup at a time into the yeast mixture. Stir until the dough comes together. Knead on a floured surface, sprinkling with additional whole wheat flour, for 8 to 10 minutes, or until the dough is fairly smooth and has lost most of its stickiness.

   Alternatively, stir the yeast and honey into the water in the bowl of an electric mixer. Let stand for 10 minutes, or until foamy. Chop the starter into small pieces and add to the dissolved yeast. Stir with the paddle until the starter is in little shreds. Add the flour and salt and mix until the dough comes together. Change to the dough hook and knead for 2 minutes at low speed and 2 minutes at medium speed. The dough should be fairly smooth and have lost most of its stickiness. Finish kneading briefly by hand on a floured surface, if you like.

Place the dough in an oiled bowl, cover tightly with plastic wrap, and let rise for 2 hours, or until doubled in bulk.

3. Turn the dough out onto a well-floured surface and shape into a loaf without punching the dough down. Place the loaf on a lightly oiled baking sheet or a peel sprinkled with cornmeal. Cover with wax paper or a kitchen towel, or lightly oil the top and cover with plastic wrap. Let rise for 45 minutes to 1 hour, or until doubled in bulk.

4. Preheat the oven to 450° F. If you are using a baking stone, put it in the oven and turn the oven on 30 minutes before baking; sprinkle the stone with cornmeal just before sliding the loaf onto it. Bake for 10 minutes, spraying three times with water. Reduce the heat to 400° F. and bake for 25 minutes more. Let cool completely on a wire rack.

This spicy-hot bread gives the Smoked Chicken and Pepper Sandwich (page 39) its distinctive flavor.

JIMMY SCHMIDT'S JALAPEÑO CHEDDAR CHEESE BREAD

Makes 2 loaves

2¼ cups warm water (110° F.)
1½ tablespoons active dry yeast
 1 tablespoon sugar
6¾ cups all-purpose flour
 1 tablespoon salt
 1 large egg, lightly beaten
 ¼ cup minced canned jalapeño peppers
1¼ cups grated cheddar cheese
 ⅛ cup corn oil

1. In a medium bowl, combine the water, yeast, and sugar. Allow to proof for 5 to 10 minutes.
2. In a mixer with a dough hook, combine the flour, salt, and egg. Add the yeast mixture. Work the dough until it is smooth and elastic. Add the peppers and cheese, and mix just until blended. Add the oil just to coat the outside of the dough. (If the dough is mixed too long at this point, the cheese will melt.) Transfer the dough to a well-oiled bowl. Let it double in bulk, at room temperature.
3. Preheat the oven to 300° F. Punch down the dough. Shape it into 2 loaves and place in lightly oiled loaf pans. Let rise until doubled in bulk. Place the loaves in the bottom third of the oven. Bake for 1 hour, or until the loaves sound hollow when tapped. Let cool on a wire rack.

GARY DANKO'S WALNUT BREAD

Makes 2 loaves

 2 tablespoons active dry yeast
 1 tablespoon honey
1½ cups lukewarm milk
 2 cups whole wheat flour
 2 cups all-purpose white flour
2½ teaspoons salt
 ¼ cup large egg whites
 ½ cup lightly toasted walnuts

1. In a large bowl, stir the yeast and honey into the milk and let stand for 5 minutes to proof. Add half of the flour and the salt and egg whites. Beat thoroughly, then add the nuts and as much of the remaining flour as is necessary for a smooth dough. Knead the dough in a heavy-duty mixer or by hand for 8 to 10 minutes, or until smooth and elastic. Put the dough in a buttered large bowl, cover, and let rise in a warm spot until doubled in bulk.

2. Punch the dough down and let it rest for 5 minutes. Butter or oil 2 loaf pans. Shape the dough into 2 loaves and place them in the pans. Cover and let rise again until doubled in bulk.

3. Preheat the oven to 375° F. Bake the bread for 45 to 50 minutes. Remove from the pans and let cool completely on a wire rack.

NOTE: This is also delicious made with toasted and skinned hazelnuts.

Herb focaccia

Makes six to eight 4-inch sandwich squares

  1 ounce active dry yeast
1⅓ cups lukewarm water
1¼ cups olive oil
5¼ cups all-purpose flour
  ¼ cup finely chopped fresh herbs (rosemary, sage, or parsley)
  1 teaspoon salt
  1 tablespoon coarse salt

This recipe for the chewy Italian flatbread focaccia is one of the best I have ever eaten. (Fougasse of France is a close relative.) This is another recipe from the Model Bakery in St. Helena. Delicious flavored with sage or parsley; irresistible with rosemary.

1. In a large mixing bowl, dissolve the yeast in ½ cup of the water. Let it proof for 10 minutes. Add ¼ cup of the olive oil and the flour, herbs, salt, and remaining water to make a soft dough. Knead in an electric mixer with a dough hook or by hand for 5 minutes, or until smooth and elastic, adding a little more flour to prevent sticking. Oil the large mixing bowl, without washing it, and turn the dough several times to coat it. Cover with a damp clean kitchen towel or plastic wrap and put in a warm place, away from drafts, for 1½ to 2 hours, or until doubled in bulk.

2. Punch down the dough and return it to the bowl. Coat it with olive oil and let it rise for 20 to 30 minutes more, or until light.

3. Preheat the oven to 400° F. Flatten the dough by hand onto a 13 x 18-inch oiled baking sheet. Sprinkle with coarse salt. Bake for 20 minutes, or until golden brown. Brush the focaccia with oil after baking. When the bread has cooled, cut it into 4-inch squares for sandwiches.

SPREADS AND SAUCES

Here are the recipes for the sauces and spreads that go with so many of the sandwiches in this book. Together they constitute a collection of some really sumptuous add-ons, some with spice, some with fire, some velvety, some sweet, and all well worth the effort required to put them together.

Often it is a spread or a sauce or a dressing that sends a sandwich into the stratosphere. When you sauce or dress a sandwich, you are adding to the sum of its flavors while ensuring that it remains moist and juicy. A spread will do this, too, but it performs another important function: a good spread with the consistency of softened butter, if carried carefully to the edges of the sandwich, will protect the bread from the soggies even as it rules out any bone-dry mouthfuls — all told, a neat trick. Sauces, dressings, and spreads all add depth and interest of their own while, at the same time, they help develop the other flavors in a sandwich, picking up the tastes in the bread and filling until the whole is melded into a fine intensity. Sometimes they take pride of place: a smoky chilpotle puree, pungent aïoli, or spicy barbecue sauce

A recent poll of American sandwich eaters turned up the unsurprising fact that the national cold cut sandwich of choice is the ham sandwich, followed closely by the BLT. "Sandwiches Across America," a survey undertaken by the National Live-Stock and Meat Board, further disclosed that white bread barely outstrips wheat bread as our favorite sandwich bread, and lettuce, mayo, and cheese reign supreme as favorite "toppings." But we are not all of us so predictable. Survey participants cite "corned beef, beets and oranges," "ham and radishes," and "bologna, grape jelly, pickles and peanut butter" among their most-treasured combinations.

happily dominates whatever it comes in contact with. As a rule, though, spreads and dressings should enhance, not overpower.

Sweet butter, cream cheese, and peanut butter are the yeoman spreads, just as homemade mayonnaise is the basic all-around dressing. Suffused with the right herbs, condiments, or spices, as a group they start to become very interesting. Here, one realizes, is a way of incorporating complementary flavors without adding bulk. Beyond the basics, there is a whole world of mustards, flavored and compound butters, nut butters, chutneys, piquant and aromatic sour cream and yogurt combinations, and a multitude of mayonnaise derivatives, including that pillar of the delicatessen trade, good old Russian dressing.

So get out your food processor or blender and toss some of these together. They are not-so-secret weapons that work wonders, in a moment raising the prosaic to the extraordinary.

Aïoli

Makes 2 cups

3 large egg yolks, at room temperature
4 to 6 garlic cloves, peeled and pressed
⅓ teaspoon salt
Juice of ½ lemon, strained
1 cup vegetable oil or very light olive oil
3 to 4 tablespoons warm water
Freshly ground white pepper to taste

1. Mix the egg yolks, garlic, salt, and lemon juice in a blender or food processor or by hand until well blended, thick, and creamy.
2. Dribble in one-third of the oil a little at a time, blending all the while, until the sauce thickens. Gradually add the remaining oil until all is incorporated; the sauce will be quite thick.
3. Thin the mayonnaise with warm water. Correct the seasoning, adding more salt or lemon juice and a little pepper.

VARIATION

Lemon Aïoli

Add the finely grated zest of 1 lemon to the finished aïoli.

Excellent for all fish and shellfish or as a dip for blanched vegetables.

Chilpotle puree

Makes ¾ cup

1 7-ounce can roasted chilpotle peppers in tomato sauce (found in the Mexican food section of grocery stores)
2 tablespoons vegetable oil
1 teaspoon freshly squeezed lime juice

In a food processor or blender, puree the peppers with the oil and lime juice to a smooth paste. Leftover puree will keep in a sealed jar in the refrigerator for up to 2 weeks, or it can be frozen.

Simple—and super-hot. Adds real fire to the Santa Fe Grilled Cheese (page 30).

Santa Fe Grilled Cheese with Chilpotle Chili Puree and Avocado.

Opposite: Grilled Tuna Sandwich from Judy Rogers's Zuni Cafe in San Francisco.

Use this on all grilled foods, especially chicken and pork. See Uncle Bill's Pork Barbecue Sandwich (page 58).

UNCLE BILL'S BARBECUE SAUCE

Makes 2 cups

½ medium onion, finely chopped
2 garlic cloves, minced
4 tablespoons unsalted butter
1 cup ketchup
½ cup water
¼ cup cider vinegar
2 tablespoons dark brown sugar
1 tablespoon prepared mustard
   Salt
1 teaspoon freshly ground black pepper
1 teaspoon hot pepper sauce
   Lemon juice (optional)

1. Cook the onion and garlic in the butter until soft but not browned. Add the ketchup, water, vinegar, sugar, mustard, salt, pepper, and hot pepper sauce. Bring to a boil and simmer for 10 minutes.
2. Remove from the heat and let cool to room temperature. Correct the seasoning with a little lemon juice or more salt or pepper. Store in the refrigerator; best used the next day.

"We North Carolinians, of course, know — we are not taught, we are born knowing — that barbecue consists of pork cooked over hickory coals and seasoned with vinegar and red pepper pods. No serious Tarheel barbecue chef would disclose his or her preferred proportions of the latter ingredients; 'season to taste' is the proper commandment. But here's a tip: you want one and a half quarts of vinegar, seasoned to taste with red pepper, for a 65-pound pig."

Tom Wicker, NEW YORK TIMES, *1983*

RUSSIAN DRESSING

Makes 1 cup

¾ cup homemade Mayonnaise (page 119) or good store-bought mayonnaise
½ tablespoon prepared horseradish, drained
¼ cup finely chopped cold cooked beets
½ teaspoon grated onion
½ teaspoon Worcestershire sauce
½ tablespoon caviar (optional)

This gets its pink color from chopped beets rather than the more usual tomato ketchup. An important ingredient in the Pastrami Reuben (page 51).

Mix the mayonnaise, horseradish, and beets until light pink. Add the onion and Worcestershire sauce and mix thoroughly. Fold in the caviar gently. Refrigerate for at least 1 hour.

Mayonnaise

Makes 2 cups

3 large egg yolks, parboiled for 3 minutes (discard white)
2 teaspoons Dijon mustard
1 tablespoon vinegar (sherry, red wine, tarragon, champagne, or rice)
1 teaspoon coarse salt
   Pinch of white or black pepper
2¼ cups vegetable oil or very light olive oil

Basic to the life of a multitude of sandwiches.

1. Beat the egg yolks with a whisk or in a food processor or blender until light and lemon-colored. Add the mustard, vinegar, salt, and pepper.
2. Beat in the oil drop by drop until it begins to thicken. Continue pouring in a steady stream, beating, until all of the oil is incorporated.

VARIATIONS

Basil Mayonnaise

Add ½ cup finely chopped fresh basil leaves to the finished mayonnaise.

Mustard Mayonnaise Jimmy Schmidt

Substitute the juice of 2 lemons for the vinegar. Add 2 tablespoons paprika, ¼ cup finely chopped chives, and ¼ cup finely chopped cilantro.

Sage Mayonnaise Robert Kinkead

Substitute 1 tablespoon honey mustard for the Dijon mustard and add ¼ cup finely chopped fresh sage leaves.

Watercress Mayonnaise

Use champagne vinegar, and add ½ cup finely chopped watercress to the finished mayonnaise.

Lemon Mayonnaise Arcadia

Substitute the vinegar with the juice of 1½ lemons, strained, and add the grated zest of 1 lemon.

HORSERADISH MAYONNAISE

Makes 1 cup

½ cup homemade Mayonnaise (page 119) or good store-bought
    mayonnaise
½ cup sour cream
¼ cup finely grated fresh horseradish or well-drained prepared
    horseradish
1 teaspoon Dijon mustard
¼ teaspoon salt
    Freshly ground white pepper to taste (I like lots)

Combine the mayonnaise, sour cream, horseradish, mustard, salt,
and pepper in a small bowl, stirring to blend thoroughly. Covered
and kept refrigerated, the mixture can be made several days in advance. Drain off any liquid that may form as it sits.

SALSA MAYONNAISE CAFFÈ QUADRO

Makes 2 cups

2 large egg yolks
2 cups olive oil
2 tablespoons lemon juice
½ teaspoon salt
1 tablespoon finely pureed or mashed garlic
2 tablespoons grated lemon zest
1 tablespoon freshly ground black pepper
6 tablespoons finely minced white onion
3 tablespoons finely minced jalapeño peppers (less if they are
    very hot)

1. Whisk together the egg yolks and 1 to 2 tablespoons oil. Then
gradually whisk in the remaining oil, drop by drop, to make
mayonnaise.
2. Add the lemon juice, salt, garlic, lemon zest, and black pepper.
Fold in the onion and jalapeños.

Rémoulade sauce

Makes 1 cup

1 cup finely diced raw vegetables (cauliflower, carrots, onions)

Marinade

½ cup white wine vinegar
1 cup water
½ cup sugar

1 large egg yolk
2 tablespoons sweet mustard
1 tablespoon light brown sugar
1 tablespoon white wine vinegar
½ cup vegetable or olive oil
  Salt and pepper to taste
2 tablespoons finely chopped cornichon pickles

1. Plunge the vegetables into boiling water, removing them as soon as the water returns to a boil. Drain well and set aside in a medium mixing bowl.
2. Make the marinade in a small saucepan: heat the vinegar, water, and sugar, stirring several times, until the sugar dissolves. Pour over the vegetables and marinate overnight.
3. In a food processor or blender, blend the egg yolk with the mustard, sugar, and vinegar. Slowly add the oil in a steady stream to make a thick mayonnaise. Season with salt and pepper. Drain the vegetables and mix them in, along with pickles. Rémoulade sauce can be made several days in advance and refrigerated.

This sauce has a special affinity with fish and especially the Pynet Rodspaette smörrebrod (page 78).

TAHINI SAUCE

Makes ½ cup

2 garlic cloves, peeled
   Salt to taste
¼ cup tahini (ground sesame seeds)
¼ cup fresh lemon juice
4 tablespoons cold water

In a blender or food processor, puree the garlic with the salt. Add the tahini and lemon juice and blend to a smooth paste. Add the water a little at a time to thin the sauce.

BABA GHANOUSH

Makes 2 cups

1 medium eggplant, roasted and turned under a hot broiler
     until the skin is charred all over and the pulp is soft
1 garlic clove, finely chopped
3 tablespoons fresh lemon juice
½ teaspoon salt
1 tablespoon minced fresh parsley
1 tablespoon minced fresh dill

Discard the charred skin of the eggplant. In a food processor or blender, combine the eggplant pulp with the remaining ingredients and blend until smooth. Baba ghanoush can be made a day in advance and refrigerated.

An excellent dip for bread, fish, or eggplant. Make it a constant companion to Falafel (page 70).

This rich cream is sometimes referred to as poor man's caviar. The harmony of flavors and its seductive texture will tell you why. Serve it as a dip for raw vegetables, on crackers or bread, or as a sauce for Falafel Pita Sandwich (page 70).

A favorite dressing for all fish dishes. I grew up eating it on the Chesapeake Bay Soft-Shell Crab Sandwich (page 46).

TARTAR SAUCE

Makes 1 cup

1 cup homemade Mayonnaise (page 119) or good store-bought
    mayonnaise
1½ tablespoons finely minced shallots or mild onion
2 tablespoons finely chopped dill or sweet pickle
1 tablespoon finely chopped fresh parsley
1 teaspoon lemon juice
⅛ teaspoon cayenne pepper
    Freshly ground black pepper to taste

Combine the ingredients in a small bowl, mix well, cover, and chill for 1 hour.

Rómesco sauce is one of the most popular and delicious sauces in Spanish cooking. Traditionally it is served as an accompaniment to all grilled fish and shellfish. Try it on the Tapawich (page 73).

RÓMESCO SAUCE

Makes ½ cup

1 dried ancho pepper, soaked in warm water for 1 hour, seeded
    and minced
1 small serrano pepper (½-inch long), minced (optional)
1 medium tomato, broiled for 5 minutes, peeled, seeded, and
    coarsely chopped
3 cloves garlic, minced
¼ cup blanched, skinless almonds, roasted for 3 to 5 minutes at
    350° F.
¼ cup hazelnuts, roasted for 3 to 5 minutes at 350° F., then
    gently rubbed in a clean towel to remove their skins
2 tablespoons, minced cilantro
1 slice lightly toasted crusty French bread
1 teaspoon sherry vinegar
2 to 3 tablespoons Spanish olive oil

In a food processor or blender puree all the ingredients except the olive oil to a smooth paste. Gradually add the oil in a thin stream to make a thick paste.

CLARIFIED BUTTER

Makes 1 cup

1 cup (2 sticks) unsalted butter, cut into small pieces

Melt the butter over moderate heat. Skim off all of the foam that rises to the top and discard it. Pour the clear yellow liquid into a storage container with a lid and refrigerate until ready to use. Clarified butter will keep for weeks in the refrigerator.

This clear, golden liquid burns less easily than ordinary butter. A must for all pressed or grilled sandwiches.

AVOCADO-TOMATO SALSA

Makes 2 cups

 1 teaspoon cumin seed, dry roasted in a small skillet until
       golden and fragrant, about 1 minute
 1 garlic clove, peeled and finely chopped
 ½ tablespoon lime juice
 ½ teaspoon finely chopped jalapeño pepper
 ¼ cup finely chopped scallions
       Salt and freshly ground black pepper to taste
 1 tablespoon chopped fresh coriander
 ½ pint cherry tomatoes, or ripe tomatoes, finely chopped
 ½ small ripe avocado, preferably Haas, peeled, pitted, and
       finely chopped

In a medium-size bowl, combine the cumin, garlic, lime juice, jalapeño pepper, scallions, salt and pepper to taste, and coriander. Add the tomatoes and the avocado. Mash to a chunky texture, cover and let stand at room temperature for 1 hour to allow the flavors to develop.

There are infinite variations for salsa but here is a really good one. Ideally suited for the Mexican Torta de Pavo (page 69), or serve with Tortilla Corn Chips (page 140).

SIDE ORDERS

Throughout this book I have emphasized the beauty of the sandwich as a meal-in-one. Of course a good sandwich can stand alone. That's its job, to be self-contained, a handy model of self-sufficiency. However, there's no denying that certain of the sandwich tribe like a little company. In some cases, a symbiotic relationship has developed between sandwich and side order, and the presence of a particular side order can become all but mandatory if this affinity has etched itself strongly in the public mind. After all, deli loves a sour pickle, a burger fresh from the summer grill gets really comfortable only if it's accompanied by a flaky heap of potato chips, and a pungent barbecue sandwich feels undressed without some hush puppies and creamy coleslaw nestled at its side.

Though it can dress up the look of a plate with its texture and color, a good side order is not a mere decorative grace note. I see it instead as something additional and complementary that's really delicious. Most side orders, both old-fashioned and newfangled, combine admirably with a wide variety of disparate sandwiches. If you have a little time to produce, let's say, some first-rate classic tortilla chips or surprisingly spiced onion rings

"There's cold chicken inside it,' replied the Rat briefly; 'cold-tongue cold ham cold beef pickled gherkins salad french rolls cress sandwiches potted meat ginger beer lemonade soda-water —'

"'Oh stop, stop,' cried the Mole in ecstasies. This is too much!'"

Kenneth Grahame,
WIND IN THE WILLOWS

129

to go with almost any sandwich of grilled meat or melted cheese, people are going to love you for it. There's a whole world of chips out there, and it's an easy one to master. Try the homemade Saratoga Chips (page 142) and carry over the method to other chip material: things like sweet potatoes or parsnips. Introduce your friends and family to some of the more unexpected side orders in this section, which could become as beloved and necessary as that old recipe for potato salad you were tired of making.

There are so many winning complements for sandwiches that I have felt ruthless in cutting out some of the more familiar sandwich sidekicks that you and your family may cherish. I have simply chosen to go with the extras — some uptown, some downhome — that I find myself making again and again. The ones I like most generally have the ability to surprise and refresh, adding a dollop of zest and interest to the meal. Here, then, is a best-of-the-best assortment to go along with your home-grown sandwich constructs. Make more than you think you'll need. People will unfailingly consume these supposed "second thoughts" in quantities exceeding all expectations.

CHILI CON CARNE

Serves 6 to 8

3 dried ancho peppers, seeded and stemmed
2 tablespoons vegetable oil
2 pounds rump roast or beef chuck, cut into small cubes
1 small to medium onion, finely chopped
3 garlic cloves, minced
4 ounces tomato sauce
2 fresh serrano peppers, halved and seeded
1 jalapeño pepper, halved and seeded
1 tablespoon tomato paste
3½ tablespoons chili powder
1 tablespoon hot paprika
1 tablespoon ground cumin
½ teaspoon cayenne pepper
½ tablespoon salt
1 ounce beer

1. Simmer the anchos in 3 cups water for 15 to 20 minutes, or until reconstituted. Remove the anchos, reserving the liquid. Discard the skin from the anchos and puree the flesh.
2. Put the oil, beef, onion, and garlic in a large pot and cook over medium heat until lightly browned. Add the reserved ancho liquid and the tomato sauce and chilies. Simmer, uncovered, for 1 hour, stirring at least once.
3. Remove the chili pieces, add the remaining ingredients in the order listed, and simmer for 45 minutes to 1 hour. If the chili becomes too dry, add a little water during the cooking.

A sound all-around chili to serve on hamburgers or frankfurters. No beans, please.

Robert Kinkead's Thanksgiving on a Bun from 21 Federal in Washington, D.C.

CORN BREAD PECAN STUFFING

Makes 1 quart

½ pound bacon, diced
¼ pound Smithfield ham, diced
1 large onion, diced
3 celery stalks, diced
¼ cup chopped fresh sage or 2 tablespoons dried sage
4 cups chicken or turkey stock
1 bay leaf
4 cups corn bread, cubed and dried
1 pound pork sausage links, browned and diced
½ cup toasted and coarsely chopped pecans
¼ cup maple syrup
    Salt and pepper to taste
1 teaspoon unsalted butter

1. In a medium heavy-based saucepan, sauté the bacon until most of the fat is rendered and the bacon is crisp. Add the ham, onion, and celery and sauté until the onion is clear but not browned. Stir in the sage and add the stock and bay leaf. Bring to a boil, then cook over high heat until reduced by one-third. Add the corn bread, sausage, pecans, and maple syrup and mix together. It should be somewhat moist. Remove from the heat. Season with salt and pepper.
2. Preheat the oven to 350° F. Butter the bottom of a small casserole dish. Put the stuffing in the dish. Top with a few dabs of butter, cover with foil, and bake for 15 to 20 minutes, or until the sides of the stuffing are bubbling. If you desire a crisp topping, remove the foil for the last 5 minutes of baking.

No Thanksgiving would be complete without stuffing; here is a first-rate version. Layer it on the Thanksgiving on a Bun (page 34) for true ambrosia.

CRANBERRY SAUCE ROBERT KINKEAD

Makes ¾ cup

1 pound fresh cranberries
    Zest and juice of 1 orange
½ cup white wine
¼ cup maple syrup, or to taste

Combine all of the ingredients in a heavy-based saucepan. Bring to a boil, then cook over medium heat, stirring occasionally, until the cranberries just begin to pop. Remove from the heat, set aside to cool, cover, and refrigerate.

A maple-flavored cranberry sauce for Thanksgiving or the day after, piled on the Thanksgiving on a Bun (page 34).

Lawrence Vito's excellent potato salad, found at the Stanford Court in San Francisco.

SPICY NEW POTATO SALAD

Serves 10

Dressing

  1 cup homemade Mayonnaise (page 119) or good store-bought mayonnaise
  ½ cup sour cream
  ½ cup finely diced smoked country-style ham
1½ tablespoons sugar
  1 teaspoon salt
  1 tablespoon red wine vinegar
  1 teaspoon Dijon mustard
    Dash of cayenne pepper

  3 pounds small red new potatoes
  1 tablespoon salt

1. Mix all of the dressing ingredients in a bowl.
2. Cover the potatoes with 3 inches of water, add the salt, and simmer gently until just cooked through. Let cool, then quarter and toss with the dressing.

There are dozens of uses for America's favorite condiment, but surely no hamburger would be complete without it. This version is from Lawrence Vito.

KETCHUP

Makes 2 quarts

15 pounds large vine-ripened tomatoes, chopped
  2 medium peppers, seeded and chopped
1½ cups cider vinegar
1¼ cups dark brown sugar
  2 teaspoons coarse salt
  1 tablespoon ground allspice
  1 tablespoon ground cloves
  ½ teaspoon cayenne pepper
  1 teaspoon ground ginger
  1 teaspoon freshly ground black pepper
  ½ teaspoon dry mustard

1. In a stainless-steel saucepan, cook the tomatoes over medium heat, stirring frequently to prevent sticking. When very soft, strain through a food mill or strainer; only the seeds and skin should remain behind.
2. Combine all of the remaining ingredients with the tomatoes in the saucepan and reduce over medium heat for approximately 1 hour, to a consistency slightly thinner than that of store-bought ketchup.

TANGY TARHEEL COLESLAW

Serves 6 to 8

- 1 medium head cabbage, shredded (about 2 pounds)
- 2 teaspoons salt
- ½ large onion, very finely chopped
- ½ cup finely grated carrot
- 3 tablespoons minced fresh parsley
- ½ cup homemade Mayonnaise (page 119) or good store-bought mayonnaise
- 1 teaspoon dry mustard
- ½ cup sour cream
- 3 tablespoons cider vinegar
- 1 teaspoon freshly ground black pepper
- 2 tablespoons sugar

Combine the cabbage, salt, onion, carrot, and parsley and toss to coat with salt. Mix together the remaining ingredients and blend thoroughly with the vegetables. Correct the seasoning, adding salt and pepper to taste. Let stand in a cool place for 30 minutes to 1 hour for a more wilted slaw; toss again and serve.

These crisp cornmeal fritters are the classic accompaniment to the barbecue sandwich (page 58) and many other southern dishes.

HUSH PUPPIES

Serves 6

1½ cups yellow cornmeal
½ cup all-purpose flour
1 teaspoon salt
1 teaspoon sugar
1 tablespoon baking powder
1 teaspoon baking soda
¼ teaspoon freshly ground black pepper
2 to 3 tablespoons minced scallions
2 large eggs, beaten
1 cup buttermilk
2 tablespoons melted lard or vegetable shortening
Peanut oil for deep frying

1. Sift all of the dry ingredients together into a large mixing bowl. Make a well in the center and add the scallions, eggs, buttermilk, and lard. Stir well.
2. In a deep fryer or wok, heat the oil to 375° F. Drop the batter by the heaping teaspoonful into the oil. The hush puppies will sink to the bottom, rise to the top, and turn a light golden color. When golden brown (3 to 5 minutes; do not overbrown them), remove with a slotted spoon and drain on crumpled paper towels. Serve at once, or keep warm in a slow oven.

Refried beans take a little time to prepare but are certainly well worth the effort. Offer these on the Torta de Pavo (page 69).

FRIJOLES REFRITOS

Serves 6 to 8

3 tablespoons lard or vegetable shortening
½ medium onion, finely chopped
3 to 4 cups cooked black beans with broth

1. Heat the lard in a large heavy frying pan and sauté the onion until translucent but not browned.
2. Add 1 cup of beans at a time to the onion, mashing them and cooking over high heat until they start to dry out and sizzle. The beans are ready when they are cooked dry (about 15 to 20 minutes).

Hushpuppies with Tartar Sauce

The best French fries in the world, naturally, are found in France. This recipe comes from one of the best teachers and chefs that this country has to offer.

MADELEINE KAMMAN'S FRITES À LA PARISIENNE

Serves 6

6 very large russet potatoes
3 quarts grape-seed oil
    Salt

1. Peel the potatoes. Do not make large holes to remove the eyes; rather, pass the peeler lightly over each eye until it has been erased. Cut the potatoes into slices ¼ to ⅓ inch thick, then recut each slice into sticks ¼ to ⅓ inch wide. Put the sticks in a colander and wash them under cold running water until the runoff shows no traces of whitish starch. Spread the potatoes in a single layer over several kitchen towels. Dry them completely.
2. In a deep fryer, heat the oil to 375° F. Put 3 to 4 handfuls of potatoes in a deep-frying basket. Immerse it in the hot oil and cook until a thin pale yellow crust builds around the potato sticks. Remove to crumpled paper towels. Repeat with the remaining potatoes.
3. Raise the temperature of the oil to between 425° and 450° F. or until the oil shows the first signs of smoking. Add half of the potatoes, and *be careful* — in a matter of seconds they will be golden and crisp. Do not overbrown them. Remove them immediately to clean crumpled paper towels and salt them. Cook the second batch. Serve within a few minutes.

VARIATION

Sweet Potato Fries

Robert Kinkead substitutes sweet potatoes for regular potatoes and serves them with his Thanksgiving on a Bun (page 34).

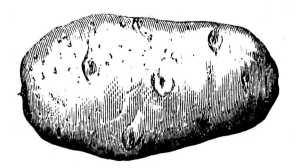

ONION RINGS

Serves 4 to 6

Buttermilk Batter

    1 large egg
    1 cup buttermilk
    ¼ teaspoon Tabasco sauce (optional)
    1 cup all-purpose flour
    ½ teaspoon salt
    ½ teaspoon baking soda

Crisp-Fried Onion Coating

    1 cup all-purpose flour
    ½ teaspoon salt
    ¼ teaspoon freshly ground black pepper
    1 tablespoon fresh herbs or 1 teaspoon dried herbs or spices,
        singly or in combination: thyme, rosemary, sage, oregano,
        curry powder, cumin, cayenne pepper, fennel seed, to
        mention a few
    3 to 4 large onions (about 2 pounds). For a special treat try
        Walla Walla, Vidalia, or Maui onions
       Peanut oil for deep frying
       Coarse salt

1. Cut the onions into very thin slices. Separate into rings. Soak the onions in ice water for 1 hour.

2. Make the buttermilk batter or crisp coating. For the batter, beat together the egg, buttermilk, and Tabasco. Sift together the dry ingredients and stir in until the batter is light. Let stand for at least 1 hour. Stir again before using.

   For the crisp coating, combine all of the ingredients on a large plate or a sheet of wax paper.

3. Heat the oil to 375° F. Remove the onion rings from the water, dry thoroughly, dip in the batter or the seasoned flour, and fry in the oil, a few at a time. Remove from the oil when golden brown (about 5 minutes). The oil temperature will drop when the onions are added, then rise as the onions cook; regulate the heat accordingly. Drain on paper towels, sprinkle with coarse salt, and serve at once.

A runner-up to the French fry as the most popular sandwich accompaniment is the onion ring, especially with hamburgers. Like all other deep-fried foods, it runs the risk of being less than superb—greasy and heavy—unless properly prepared. In its glory, it is crisp, tender, and pungent. Onion rings can be dipped in either an egg-buttermilk batter or a seasoned flour mixture. Both are excellent.

A snap to make, and far superior to the overly fatty and salty commercial variety. Pair with the Mexican Torta de Pavo (page 69) and serve with Avocado-Tomato Salsa (page 127).

TORTILLA CORN CHIPS

Makes 80 chips

1 **package corn tortillas
    Peanut oil for frying
    Coarse salt**

1. Stack the tortillas in an even pile. With a sharp heavy knife, cut the stack in half, then into quarters, then into eighths. Separate the pieces.
2. In a deep fryer or wok, heat the oil to 375° F.; do not let it smoke. Fry the corn chips in small batches for 1½ to 2 minutes, stirring all the time. Remove with a slotted spoon and drain on paper towels. Repeat until all are cooked. Sprinkle with salt and serve warm.

    Stored in an airtight container, tortilla chips will keep up to 1 week. They can be made crisp again by heating in a slow oven for several minutes.

VARIATION

To lower the calorie count, use a pastry brush to paint the corn chips with a light coating of oil. Arrange them on a lightly oiled baking sheet. Bake in a 350° F. oven for 10 minutes, or until they are crisp and just beginning to brown. Toss with coarse salt.

Onion Rings

In Thailand there is no ketchup, so the Thais put ripe tomatoes and onions right on top of the fries.

Potato chips come in all sizes and flavors, from the ruffled and ridged stand-bys to the newer Cajun- and taco-flavored varieties. I am a purist and like a lightly salted thick potato chip. The best commercially made potato chips come not from the mainland, but from the Hawaiian Islands. If you are mad for chips, forget the leis and bring back as many bags of the peerless Hawaiian chips as you can, for there is no match anywhere for their thick, crisp texture and sweet taste.

In a wide-ranging, guilt-ridden sampling of the nationally available brands, my taste panel liked best Granny Goose Hawaiian-style potato chips, made in Oakland, California, and sold in most grocery stores, and Kettle Chips, a natural, "gourmet-style" potato chip that is thicker and less salty than most. But for a truly ambrosial experience you must make your own.

From Sal Petrolino, executive chef at the Morgan Hotel in New York City, comes this recipe for some of the best potato chips I have even eaten. Idaho potatoes are the potatoes of choice because of their perfect combination of high moisture and low sugar.

SARATOGA CHIPS

U.S. #1 Idaho potatoes, newly harvested, firm, not soft
Peanut oil for deep frying
Coarse salt to taste

1. Peel the potatoes and slice them paper-thin in a food processor, on the #5 setting of a slicing machine, or by hand. Let them rest in ice-cold water for 3 minutes. Dry in a salad spinner or on kitchen towels.
2. In a deep fryer, heat the oil to 240° F. Cook the potatoes until golden. Season with salt and serve at once.

Jimmy Schmidt's Jalapeño Potato Chips:

Add 2 to 3 whole, dried hot peppers to the oil in the deep fryer. Heat the oil to 240° F. Remove the peppers with a slotted spoon and discard. Fry the potatoes according to previous recipe.

GARLIC DILL PICKLE

Makes 4 quarts

What would most sandwiches be without a pickle! This one is mildly hot and spicy, with plenty of crunch.

8 to 9 pounds 3- to 5-inch pickling cucumbers

Brine

1 cup coarse salt
1 gallon cool water

3 cups apple cider vinegar
4½ cups water
2 tablespoons sugar
1 tablespoon mixed pickling spices
2½ tablespoons mustard seed
4 garlic cloves
12 small bunches dill
4 small hot peppers

1. Wash the cucumbers thoroughly. Discard any with blemishes or soft spots. Mix the coarse salt and 1 gallon water. Cover the cucumbers with the brine and let stand overnight. Rinse and drain the cucumbers. Discard the brine.

2. In a saucepan, mix together the vinegar, 4½ cups water, remaining salt, and the sugar. Add the pickling spices, tied in a cheesecloth bag, and bring to a boil.

3. Pack the cucumbers into 4 wide-mouth quart canning jars to within ½ inch of the top. Put 2 teaspoons mustard seed, 1 garlic clove, 3 bunches of dill, and 1 hot pepper in each jar. Cover the cucumbers with hot pickling liquid. Put the lid on the jars and screw the bands tight. Process in a boiling water bath for 20 minutes from when the jars first go into the boiling water. Let cool and store in a cool dark place. The pickles can be eaten immediately but are best if allowed to mellow for at least a week.

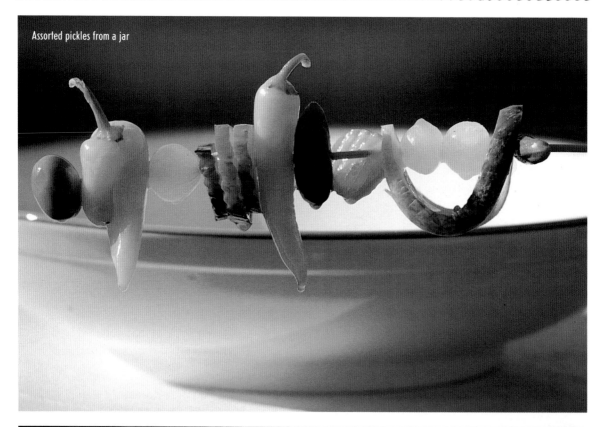

Assorted pickles from a jar

Homemade chips

BREAD AND BUTTER PICKLES

Makes 1 gallon

10 cucumbers
 8 carrots, peeled and sliced ¼ inch thick
 3 heads cauliflower, separated into florets
12 medium onions, cut into ¼-inch-thick slices
 1 tray of ice cubes
⅓ cup coarse salt
 2 cups light brown sugar
1½ teaspoons celery seed
 1 tablespoon mustard seed
 3 cups cider vinegar
1½ tablespoons turmeric

1. Using a small knife, peel the cucumbers lengthwise in 1⁄16-inch alternating strips to create a striped effect. Cut the cucumbers into slices ¼ inch thick. Place all of the vegetables in a stainless-steel, glass, or plastic container (not aluminum). Cover with water and the ice cubes and salt, and mix. Refrigerate for 16 hours, then drain thoroughly. Rinse in fresh water and let drain for 3 minutes.

2. Combine the remaining ingredients in a 1-gallon stainless-steel pot. Simmer for 1 minute. Add the vegetables and simmer at just below a boil for 5 minutes.

3. Store in special pickling or canning jars as directed by the manufacturer.

A favorite recipe for pickled vegetables, very pretty and exceptionally flavorful. They are always found as the garnish to Lawrence Vito's sandwiches and burgers at the Stanford Court.

INDEX

Page numbers in *italics* refer to illustrations.

Aïoli, 115
  grilled tuna sandwich, 31, *116*
aïoli, lemon, 115
  lobster roll with artichokes and,
    52
artichokes, lobster roll with lemon
    aïoli and, 52
asparagus and eggs sandwich,
    64, 66
avocado, Santa Fe grilled cheese
    with chilpotle chili puree and,
    30, *32*, *116*
avocado-tomato salsa, 127
  torta de pavo, 69

Baba ghanoush, 125
  falafel pita sandwich, *68*, 70
bacon:
  Brown Hotel's hot brown, 50
  Fourth Street Grill's BLT, 34
  lobster club, *x*, 35
  pressed sandwich, *33*, 35
bagel, Eli Zabar's raspberry tower
    of, *81*, 82
bannock bread, *101*, 106
  Chippewa salmon sandwich,
    48

basil mayonnaise, 119
beef:
  the best burger, 36
  Brazilian churrasco steak
    sandwich, *65*, 67
  Carlo Middione's steak fingers,
    19
  chili con carne, 131
  Ed Debevic's sloppy José, *56*,
    57
  roasted fillet of, with
    horseradish mayonnaise,
    garlic puree, and watercress
    on poppy-seed rolls, 79
black-eyed Susans, *89*, 90–91
BLT, Fourth Street Grill's, 34
bolillos, 103
bread, 97–111
  bannock, *101*, 106
  bolillos, 103
  brioche Arcadia, 106–107
  City Restaurant's garlic naan,
    104
  corn, pecan stuffing, 133
  cornmeal, Model Bakery, 107
  Gary Danko's walnut, 110–111
  herb focaccia, 111

  Jimmy Schmidt's jalapeño
    cheddar cheese, 110
  pane integrale con miele,
    108–109
  sandwich or burger buns, *100*,
    102
breakfast sandwiches:
  Debbie Schneider's strata, *88*,
    91
  Eli Zabar's raspberry tower of
    bagel, *81*, 82
  French toast, 92
  sourdough, with peach pecan
    butter sauce, *84*, 95
brioche Arcadia, 106–107
  brioscie al gelato, 94–95
  lobster club, *x*, 35
brioscie al gelato, 94–95

brown bread and nasturtium
    sandwiches, 5, 11
burger, the best, 36
burger buns, *see* sandwich or
    burger buns
butter:
    sauce, peach pecan, sourdough
        breakfast sandwich with, *84*,
        95
    see also clarified butter

Cake, angel food, 86
cheddar cheese jalapeño bread,
    Jimmy Schmidt's, 110
    smoked chicken and pepper
        sandwich, 39
cheese:
    brown bread and nasturtium
        sandwiches, 5, 11
    blue castello, with native figs
        on toasted walnut bread, 11,
        12
    cheddar, jalapeño bread, Jimmy
        Schmidt's, 110
    French toast sandwich, 92
    grilled, with chilpotle chili puree
        and avocado, Santa Fe, 30,
        32, *116*
    grilled eggplant sandwiches,
        18
    Italian hero, grinder, or
        submarine, 58
    Jimmy Schmidt's smoked
        chicken and pepper
        sandwich, 39
    Madeleine Kamman's sandwich
        montagnard, *72*, *73*
    Monte Cristo, 75
    mozzarella in carrozza, 18–19
    muffuletta, *52*, 55
    Neapolitan sandwiches, 5, 10
    pastrami Reuben, 51
    pressed sandwich, *33*, 35
chicken:
    crostini di fegatini, 17
    pressed sandwich, *33*, 35
    smoked, and pepper sandwich,
        Jimmy Schmidt's, 39
chili con carne, 131
    Coney Island red hots, 51

chilpotle chili puree, 115
    Santa Fe grilled cheese with
        avocado and, 30, *32*, *116*
    torta de pavo, 69
chocolate:
    black-eyed Susans, *89*, 90–91
    brioscie al gelato, 94–95
    sauce, 86
clarified butter, 127
    pynet rodspaette, *77*, 78
    Santa Fe grilled cheese with
        chilpotle chili puree and
        avocado, 30, *32*
club, lobster, *x*, 35
coffee ice cream, 86
    brioscie al gelato, 94–95
coleslaw, tangy tarheel, 135
    Uncle Bill's pork barbecue
        sandwich, 58–59
Coney Island red hots, 51
cookie sandwiches:
    black-eyed Susans, *89*, 90–91
    peanut butter, 83

corn bread pecan stuffing, 133
    Thanksgiving on a bun, 34, *132*
corn chips, tortilla, 140
cornmeal:
    bread Model Bakery, 107
    hush puppies, 136, *137*
crab sandwich, soft-shell
    Chesapeake Bay, *45*, 46
cranberry sauce Robert Kinkead,
    133
    Thanksgiving on a bun, 34, *132*
cream cheese:
    brown bread and nasturtium
        sandwiches, 5, 11
    French toast sandwich, 92
    Neapolitan sandwiches, 5, 10
crostini di fegatini, *16*, 17

Dessert sandwiches:
    black-eyed Susans, *89*, 90–91
    brioscie al gelato, 94–95
    Hilary Bein's angel, *84*, *85*,
        86–87
    peanut butter, 83

Egg(s):
    and asparagus sandwich, *64*,
        66
    Neapolitan sandwiches, 5, 10
    quail, gravlax on wheat toast
        with osetra caviar and, *21*,
        22–23
    salad sandwich, Café Fanny's,
        24, 38
eggplant:
    baba ghanoush, 125
    roast lamb on garlic naan with
        onion marmalade and, 74–
        75, *76*
    sandwiches, deep-fried, *12*, 15
    sandwiches, grilled, 18

Falafel pita sandwich, *68*, 70
figs, native, with blue castello on
    toasted walnut bread, 11, *12*
finger sandwiches, 5–23
focaccia, herb, 111
    grilled tuna sandwich, 31, *116*
French toast:
    sandwich, 92
    sourdough breakfast sandwich
        with peach pecan butter
        sauce, *84*, 95
frijoles refritos, 136
    torta de pavo, 69

Garlic:
  aïoli, 115
  dill pickle, 143
  puree, roasted fillet of beef
    with horseradish mayonnaise,
    watercress and, on poppy-
    seed rolls, 79
garlic naan, City Restaurant's,
    104
roast lamb on, with eggplant
    and onion marmalade,
    74–75, *76*
gelato di nocciole, 94
gravlax on wheat toast with quail
    egg and osetra caviar, *21*,
    22–23
grilled sandwiches:
  cheese with chilpotle chili puree
    and avocado, Santa Fe, 30,
    32, *116*
  eggplant, 18
  tuna, 31, *116*
grinder, hero, or submarine,
    Italian, 58
Gruyère cheese:
  Jimmy Schmidt's smoked
    chicken and pepper
    sandwich, 39
  Monte Cristo, 75
  pastrami Reuben, 51

Hazelnut(s):
  black-eyed Susans, *89*, 90–91
  bread, Gary Danko's, 110–111
  brioscie al gelato, 94–95
herb focaccia, 111
  grilled tuna sandwich, 31, *116*
hero, grinder, or submarine,
    Italian, 58

horseradish mayonnaise, 122
  roasted fillet of beef with garlic
    puree, watercress and, on
    poppy-seed rolls, 79
hot brown, Brown Hotel's, 50
hot dogs:
  Coney Island red hots, 51
  Jody Maroni's haut dog, 29
hush puppies, 136, *137*
  Uncle Bill's pork barbecue
    sandwich, 58–59

Ice cream sandwiches:
  brioscie al gelato, 94–95
  Hilary Bein's angel, *84*, *85*,
    86–87
international sandwiches, 61–79
Italian hero, grinder, or subma-
    rine, 58

Jalapeño cheddar cheese bread,
    Jimmy Schmidt's, 110
jalapeño potato chips, Jimmy
    Schmidt's, 142

Ketchup, 134–135

Lamb, roast, on garlic naan with
    eggplant and onion marma-
    lade, *74–75*, *76*
lemon aïoli, 115
  lobster roll with artichokes and,
    52
lemon mayonnaise Arcadia, 119
  lobster club, *x*, 35
lobster:
  club, *x*, 35
  roll with lemon aïoli and
    artichokes, 52

Mayonnaise, 119
  aïoli, 115
  Fourth Street Grill's BLT, 34
  horseradish, 122
  mustard, 74
  Russian dressing, 118
  salsa, Caffè Quadro, 122
  spicy new potato salad, 134
  tangy tarheel coleslaw, 135
  tartar sauce, 126
  variations, 119
mocha gelato, 94
Monte Cristo, 75
mozzarella:
  in carrozza, 18–19
  grilled eggplant sandwiches,
    18
muffuletta, *52*, 55
mushroom, wild, sandwiches, 14

mustard mayonnaise, 74
  roast lamb on garlic naan
    with eggplant and onion
    marmalade, *74–75*, *76*
mustard mayonnaise Jimmy
    Schmidt, 119
  smoked chicken and pepper
    sandwich, 39

Nasturtium and brown bread
    sandwiches, 5, 11
Neapolitan sandwiches, 5, 10

Onion:
  marmalade, roast lamb on
    garlic naan with eggplant
    and, *74–75*, *76*
  rings, 139, *140*
oyster loaf, 54

Pan bagnat, 71
pane integrale con miele, 108–109
    brown bread and nasturtium
        sandwiches, 5, 11
    gravlax on, with quail egg and
        osetra caviar, 21, 22–23
    Italian hero, grinder, or
        submarine, 58
    wild mushroom sandwiches,
        14
pastrami Reuben, 51
peach pecan butter sauce,
    sourdough breakfast sandwich
    with, 84, 95
peanut butter cookie sandwiches,
    83
pecan:
    corn bread stuffing, 133
    peach butter sauce, sourdough
        breakfast sandwich with, 84,
        95
    Thanksgiving on a bun, 34, 132
pepper(s):
    chilpotle puree, 115, 116
    red, coulis, tartine of smoked
        salmon and, 21, 23
    and smoked chicken sandwich,
        Jimmy Schmidt's, 39
pickle, garlic dill, 143
pickles, bread and butter, 145
pita falafel sandwich, 68, 70
poor boy, shrimp Ms. Ann, 47, 48
poppy-seed rolls, roasted fillet of
        beef with horseradish may-
        onnaise, garlic puree, and
        watercress on, 79
pork:
    barbecue sandwich, Uncle
        Bill's, 58–59

Jody Maroni's haut dog, 29
potato(es):
    Madeleine Kamman's frites à
        la Parisienne, 138
    salad, spicy new, 134
potato chips:
    Jimmy Schmidt's jalapeño, 142
    Saratoga, 142
pressed sandwich, 33, 35
pynet rodspaette, 77, 78

Raspberry tower of bagel,
    Eli Zabar's, 81, 82
red hots, Coney Island, 51
regional favorites, 41–59
rémoulade sauce, 123
    pynet rodspaette, 77, 78
Reuben, pastrami, 51
rómesco sauce, 126
Russian dressing, 118
    pastrami Reuben, 51

Sage mayonnaise Robert Kinkead,
    119
salmon:
    gravlax on wheat toast with
        quail egg and osetra caviar,
        21, 22–23
    sandwich, Chippewa, 48
    smoked, tartine of red pepper
        coulis and, 21, 23
salsa, avocado-tomato, 127
salsa mayonnaise Caffè Quadro,
    122
    Brazilian churrasco steak
        sandwich, 65, 67

sandwich or burger buns, 100,
    102
    the best burger, 36
    Chesapeake Bay soft-shell crab
        sandwich, 45, 46
    Ed Debevic's sloppy José, 56,
        57
    lobster roll with lemon aïoli
        and artichokes, 52
    Uncle Bill's pork barbecue
        sandwich, 58–59

shrimp:
    Ms. Ann poor boy, 47, 48
    pynet rodspaette, 77, 78
    tapawich, 73
side orders, 129–145
    bread and butter pickles, 145
    chili con carne, 131
    corn bread pecan stuffing, 133
    cranberry sauce Robert
        Kinkead, 133
    frijoles refritos, 136
    garlic dill pickle, 143
    hush puppies, 136, 137
    ketchup, 134–135
    Madeleine Kamman's frites à
        la Parisienne, 138
    onion rings, 139, 140
    Saratoga chips, 142
    spicy new potato salad, 134
    tangy tarheel coleslaw, 135
    tortilla corn chips, 140
sloppy José, Ed Debevic's, 56, 57
sourdough breakfast sandwich
    with peach pecan butter
    sauce, 84, 95

spreads and sauces, 113–127
  aïoli, 115
  avocado-tomato salsa, 127
  baba ghanoush, 125
  chilpotle puree, 115, *116*
  chocolate sauce, 86
  clarified butter, 127
  cranberry sauce Robert
    Kinkead, 133
  dipping sauce, 15
  horseradish mayonnaise, 122
  ketchup, 134–135
  mayonnaise, 119
  rémoulade sauce, 123
  rómesco sauce, 126
  Russian dressing, 118
  salsa mayonnaise Caffè Quadro,
    122
  tahini sauce, 125
  tartar sauce, 126
  Uncle Bill's barbecue sauce,
    118

strata, Debbie Schneider's
    breakfast, *88*, 91
stuffing, corn bread pecan, 133
  Thanksgiving on a bun, 34, *132*
submarine, hero, or grinder,
    Italian, 58
sweet potato fries, 138
  Thanksgiving on a bun, 34, *132*

Tahini sauce, 125
  falafel pita sandwich, *68*, 70
tapawich, 73
tartar sauce, 126
  Chesapeake Bay soft-shell crab
    sandwich, *45*, 46
tartine of smoked salmon and red
    pepper coulis, *21*, 23
Thanksgiving on a bun, 34, *132*
tomato-avocado salsa, 127
torta de pavo, 69
tortilla corn chips, 140

tuna:
  grilled, sandwich, 31, *116*
  pan bagnat, 71
turkey:
  Brown Hotel's hot brown, 50
  Thanksgiving on a bun, 34, *132*
  torta de pavo, 69

Unsandwiches, 81–95
updated American classics, 25–39

Walnut bread, Gary Danko's,
    110–111
  toasted, native figs with blue
    castello on, 11, *12*
watercress, roasted fillet of beef
    with horseradish mayonnaise,
    garlic puree and, on poppy-
    seed rolls, 79
watercress mayonnaise, 119
  Chippewa salmon sandwich, 48